Home Shopping Diva...Lessons, Lyrics, and Lipstick

Home Shopping Diva... Lessons, Lyrics, and Lipstick

By
Meg Flather

Thank you to my husband for making me do this.

I want to thank Mathias Sanders and Carolyn Marcell Elmore for being my safe places to share each chapter when first written.

I am so grateful to Ashley Wren Collins, Amanda Maciel, Sarah LeBuhn, Sara Holmes, Dani Grunfeld, Erica Jensen, Nancy Myer, and my sister, Lisa Flather who all proofread early drafts.

A thank you to Julie Flather Zeitlin for her illustration, Maryjane Fahey for her graphic design, and Glen Nelson for editing this book.

In my book, I've retained the names of family and friends who graciously gave me permission to appear. Out of respect for my professional colleagues and others that I was unable to contact, I've changed a few names.

This book is dedicated to my young roses: may you learn a little something from your Auntie Meg, your Home Shopping Diva.

Chapter One

"So, how did you end up doing this?"

I have always loved the sound my shoes make upon tile floors. As a child I spent many hours walking down airport corridors, listening for the *click, click, click* they made on the long walk to the gate. I would listen for the echo they made in hopes of interrupting what other passengers awaiting flights were saying, reading, or doing. Each *click, click, click* would exclaim, *I am here! I am here in my fancy shoes. Can you all hear me? Are you looking at me? Look at me! I am here!*

It is March, 2010. I find myself listening for the *click, click, click* my heels now make against the tile floors of the only home shopping channel of Canada as I round the corner to the hallway of dressing rooms. One more show. I have one more show to go and then I get to go back to the hotel, watch David Letterman and have my glass of white wine with plenty of ice on the side. I also get to crawl into the clean, white, king-sized sheets that I have all to myself. This post-show fantasy is quickly interrupted by the TV monitor sounding over my head, "OK, now let's take a look at the value page to see what you are getting."

It is about 9 p.m., and I have been going since midnight. I have been selling the top value of the day: Italian crème bath, body crème, hand crème, and talc in choices of Honey, Pink Peony, Aloe & Soy, Double Latte for Sensitive Skin, and Certified & Organic Shea Butter. Each flavor comes in a complimentary colored canvas bag reflecting the choice with true style. Yellow, pink, lime green, deep blue, and coral canvas bags with product and props scattered around them sit on the selling table in the TV studio, my stage for the last 24 hours. I believe I started with 5,000 units and have a good thousand left with only one more show to go at 11 p.m. I am now taking my break.

The buyers decided to have me share my final hour with a makeup line to help us both attract new viewers. They asked if I would allow the artist who sells the brand to make me over as well. I arrive at her door. An energetic, young woman welcomes me into her dressing room. I feel suddenly old. My peri-menopausal, exhausted face has not stopped smiling for two days. See, this is the drill. I fly from Newark Airport to Toronto, landing around 5 p.m. where my driver takes me to my beloved hotel. I check in, order dinner, study my notes, and stare into the darkness of my room wishing I could nap. When the alarm finally sounds, I then shower, dress, spackle makeup on my face, attempt to control my frizzy hair, and meet the car downstairs to arrive at the studio an hour before the midnight launch of the value of the day. Except for two hours of sleep between the midnight and 7 a.m. shows, I am up for 24 hours sharing the features and benefits of Italian bath and body care with all of Canada. I am in heaven as I do this; absolute heaven.

So, the answer to the buyer was, "Yes, yes, yes! I will share the hour and yes, please make me over. I will need it."

I sit in her chair. This makeup artist is beautiful with sort of a Latin, Italian mix of features and coloring, and she is half my age. She smells so clean and her smile is sincere. When I search her glowing complexion, I cannot find one wrinkle on her face or those hollow pockets that I started getting in my late thirties. You know those hollow pockets under the eyes on either side of the nose where you cake on the concealer hoping you have fooled everyone, but you haven't. Where it looks like someone took a tiny ice cream scooper and removed all that good plump skin. Nope. She did not have those hollow pockets yet. I apologize for my dated but trusted 1980s makeup technique of defined brows (very compulsive about my brows), dark cake liner on the top lash line and deep, dramatic red lips. I make a joke that I am the Jackie O meets Roz Russell of home shopping. I am not sure she knows who Roz Russell is. Now I am really feeling peri-menopausal.

She compliments my skin. I never really sat in the sun because I always volunteered to work weekends and more hours during summer vacations. She tells me that I look really good for my age (how is 46 supposed to look?). I am starting to relax now that I see she knows what she is doing. Her soft hands are soothing to my stressed out forehead. As she pat, pat, pats the foundation into my collection of deep brow lines, I say, "Ha! Each ex-boyfriend left me with one of these!" and allow my drag queen self to surface. I make her co-workers watching from the couch laugh. Even when tired, I am a sucker for a good audience. I am "on" again. I am in heaven.

She asks me, "So, how did you end up doing this?" I look at my watch and see that we have a good two hours before we have to go on. I am flattered by the eager faces thinking I have a story worth hearing, and begin. This is the story I tell her. This is the story of Home Shopping Diva.

I'll See You

I'll see you in the ocean
Connecting different lands
The bridges that you daily crossed
To hold a brother's hand

I'll see you in all reason
All that makes us proud
The wisest words put to page
The speeches sung out loud

Everywhere
I'll see you there
Everywhere
I'll see you there
In all the many things you love
As if you're smiling from above
Everywhere
I'll see you there

I'll see you in a marriage
That kept the other warm
The steady ships that navigate
To weather every storm

I'll see you in the faces
Of the ones you raised
In all guidance,
Those generous with praise

Everywhere
I'll see you there
Everywhere
I'll see you there
In all the many things you love
As if you're smiling from above

4

Everywhere
I'll see you there

Like the sandcastle taken by the sea
That leaves behind a summer's memory
You leave behind the best in me
You leave behind the best in me

Through the darkness
I'll see you through the fear
I'll see you when it is my turn
To leave a family here

Everywhere
I'll see you there
Everywhere
I'll see you there
In all the many things you love
As if you're smiling from above

Everywhere
I'll see you there
Everywhere
I'll see you there
In all the many things you love
As if you're smiling from above

Everywhere
I'll see you there

Chapter Two

A little family history before we begin

My father was a Peace Corps director in Malaysia. I was the Peace Corps "love child," born in Baguio, The Philippines on February 14, 1964. I weighed almost ten pounds and was born with a full head of jet black hair, matching eyes and a powerful cry. I was the youngest of four. At the time Lisa was nine, Julie was six, and Roger was four.

When I came home from the hospital there was apparently a strict baby nurse to care for me. My very Sagittarian and curious brother wanted to see what all the fuss was about inside this strange bassinet. Who was this ten-pound source of giggles and cries, maker of odd smells and too much commotion? He began to poke his four-year-old finger through the rods of my crib to touch my plump skin sleeping inside. Well, a shriek, a yelp, and a ten-pound cry resounded throughout the nursery floor. In a flash the nurse came. "Get away from the baby! Get away! You're hurting the baby!" Well, the story goes that Roger's only response was, "I'm gonna break your glasses." And so a deep and meaningful connection began. Roger needed me. I needed him. We would fight and compete for the next fifteen years with the silent understanding that we could. It was safe. All those scared, dark feelings of rage and wonder would be shared between us. A deep intimacy began the moment he pinched my baby skin, an intimacy I would have the honor to cultivate and respect. He would grow to instinctively trust that I would walk every step with him and process every decision. I would grow to rely on his continual parenting and countless rescues. That poke through the crib rods was a "Hello. I have been waiting for you. You will need me and I will need you. Welcome to the family."

Then there were my two older sisters who would mother me. Julie would be the one to prepare my meals, talk about boys, bras and what I would do if I got my period at school. Her artistic talents would win me popularity as I followed in her footsteps in schools and with camp counselors. Being related to her would help combat those first day of school and camp butterflies. I would feel safe to enter her room and confess that sometimes I felt sad and I didn't know why, and that sometimes I would have a restless stirring in my belly when entering the school bus or the girls' locker room. That sometimes I would wake in the morning with a feeling of dread, accompanied by a heavy feeling in my chest. My friends were starting to shave their legs and I didn't know what to say to boys. Was I normal? She would always assure me that everything was happening as it should and that I was very normal. I would feel a tremendous sense of loss when she went away to college, on her wedding day and on the days her two beautiful children were born.

Lisa would proofread my homework and tell me that I had a good mind. She would read me stories and share her hand-me-down lipsticks with me. I would gaze at her through the crack of her bedroom door as she brushed her long, brunette hair and wonder if I would ever be as glamorous. She was the family member who encouraged me to sing, write my own music and perform from a deeper, authentic place. She would tell me that I had something original to share with the world and that I could channel my range of emotions through lyrical folk melodies. A delayed diagnosis of her mental illness would be her private cross to bear and waste too many precious hours of her life. Yet, because of her trials she would give us all permission to get help when we needed it and demand that we always tell the truth. One of the benefits of standing fourth in line was watching and learning from these older warriors who marched before me.

My first impression of my father was that he was a charismatic force and a shot of rebellion behind Ray Ban sunglasses. He had strong, liberal political opinions and could win most debates with the data he stored in his brain from hours of reading and analysis. He had no patience for generalizations or simplifications reflecting a lack of study and discipline. He was lean, driven and passionate. His eyes were intensely dark and slightly possessed. It was as if his commitment to whatever project he was focused on intensified his brown eyes and lit a flame behind the pupils. He sang beautifully in the car, made us laugh and want to be good for him. After we left the Peace Corps in 1969, he channeled that same passion into non-profit/overseas development in the 70s,

New York City real estate in the 80s, and special education in the 90s. He passed away from stage four liver and esophageal cancer on the same day and hour that JFK was assassinated.

He was a Harvard graduate who within weeks of graduation day joined the Navy during peace time to fly planes. This decision did not make his parents happy. He was expected to remain at Harvard and attend business or law school. I always felt this choice illustrated the conflict I watched him wrestle with for the 40 years we spent together. His New England privilege seemed at odds with his passion for adventure, risk and travel. He preferred the company of "the man on the street" while advocating for the union worker, the immigrant, the disabled, anyone who suffered from discrimination, sickness or poverty. Throughout his career of "changing careers" this is what Dad did. This is who Dad was.

By the time he passed away he had reconciled what he thought were two opposing forces by writing a book called, *The Boss's Son* (his father and uncle managed the Boott Mills of Lowell, Massachusetts until it closed in the 1950s.) I believe writing this book helped him go home again before it was time to truly go home. When we found him cold in his bed, just a few days after completing his manuscript, Mom noted that his face was never more at peace. We like to think he saw his parents waiting for him as he crossed to the other side and that this was the cause for his serene expression.

I was his caretaker in the nine months that he battled cancer. I got what I needed in the nick of time. He told me the story of his life, apologized for the neglect I felt, admitted that parenting was not his plan, choice or strong suit, but that it had made him a better man. Days before he died, he said that I had "made all the difference." That moment was worth everything. I feel him every day, and in some ways, I have become my father. My political views, my enjoyment of *The News Hour* on Public Television, my love for international travel, knack for real estate, saving money and preferring the company of "the man on the street" are all treasures passed down to me from my father. We have never been closer.

No one made my mother laugh like Dad. They shared an enviable chemistry and spark together. She kept him hunting and he kept her guessing. I would see him grab her behind and hear the squeal that followed. Although I did not understand it, I instinctively knew it was a good thing. Years later when I witnessed cold, distant marriage dynamics at friends' sleepovers, I would call my mother and beg to be picked up. I thought every couple shared the same spark, a spark first lit when they met at a tenth grade dance.

My father saw my mother across a crowded room. He approached her to dance as she was escaping to the ladies room. She confessed her strapless dress was falling down and if he wanted to dance, he had to hold her very close to conceal this evening gown emergency. They slow danced behind a piano that night and never stopped dancing. Their union lasted, but changed form to maintain their intense connection to each other as well as to meet their fiercely independent needs to evolve as separate souls.

They celebrated their 50th wedding anniversary in the Sloan Kettering Emergency Room during Dad's cancer battle. His doctor had called us that afternoon, alarmed at Dad's routine blood work and asked us to come in immediately for more tests. There was no party with cake, crowds or champagne. Their celebration was to hold hands while waiting for test results which brought temporary good news and euphoric relief that Dad's tumors appeared to be shrinking. The three of us went back to their apartment elated. We bought a bag of pretzels and cheap white wine and curled up in their bed recounting their wedding day. Now that is a 50th wedding anniversary in my book.

These two Gemini twins, born just three days apart, understood something about partnership. They understood that it was not about the show or what other couples did or had. They took risks together, succeeded together and failed together. They fought, made up and made love on Sunday mornings with the door locked. They traveled the globe, built three homes, raised four children and loved two grandchildren while juggling numerous careers, degrees and projects. Although I could go on and on about how I felt neglected in my youth (with sixteen years of therapy under my belt), my parents did one thing exceptionally well. They figured out how to stay together no matter what. What a gift for me to witness, study and try to master myself.

I play this game with my friends. "Who would play my mother in the movie?" The answer, of course, is Judi Dench. She would play my mother in the movie of my life. Like the award winning actress, Mom is petite and her no-nonsense wit and charm are framed perfectly by short silvered layers of hair and a flawless complexion that has always taken ten years off her actual age.

My mother in many ways is the love of my life. All roads lead to Mom. She was a fiery, rebellious little girl who was quickly removed from public school because her father was concerned that she was having too much fun swimming with the neighborhood boys in the Charles River. So, she attended a private girls school to earn straight A's, lose far too much weight and win most of the awards at graduation. Yet she was still told that she could be a nurse or a secretary and would not go to college. Mom did not want to be a nurse or a secretary. She recalls the only time that she ever saw her mother cry was the night her mother begged her father to let her go to college. No was no. So Mom took up nursing and went as far as she could with it. Although Mom says she adored her father, she fought a huge battle to prove how wrong he was about her academic potential for most of my life.

After the Peace Corps, she worked full time as a head nurse in labor and delivery, while earning her bachelor's degree through correspondence classes and night school, complete with hours of driving down lonely suburban highways. Every day was a very long day for Mom.

After we moved to New York City in 1977, Mom went to midwifery school and also earned a masters degree in counseling. Mom never stopped reaching and excelling. Dad used to tease her that she flunked retirement because she only lasted a couple of weeks after the big send-off party that we all attended. Days after Dad hung her retirement plaque on their bedroom wall, she called her old boss and asked to go back to work. She worked over forty hours a week until she was 77 years of age. Yes, she flunked retirement, but mastered an inimitable work ethic.

Mom gave me musical comedy, movies and beautifully sewn costumes for every Halloween, school and camp production. She gave me my love for Barbie, dressing up and my Victorian doll house. Mom taught me how to keep an immaculate house, an organized purse and a desk free of papers. As she talks about The Great Depression, she asks the waiter to wrap up her half eaten quesadilla to freeze for tomorrow's lunch, and teaches me in these exchanges never to take what I have for granted. Mom is a pistol of energy, excellence, discipline and consistency. Throughout my childhood she seemed perfect to the outside world. So perfect that she also gave me her calorie counting ritual to be what she called "bone thin."

Mom is my little bird who can always tell in my voice if I am really OK. She attends every show I perform, first cheering me in the darkness, then demanding that I sing her favorite song as the encore. I always comply and then follow it with an exaggerated impression of Ethel Merman playing Mama Rose in *Gypsy*. Yes, I wanted more of her growing up, but I have her today. I cherish this and am so very thankful for the time we have now. I am certain that when she leaves me my heart will break and never recover.

On the Second Floor

A flight of stairs
A tiled floor
A woman sits
Beyond a door
I fall apart
I just begin
As laughter lets me in

Details drift
As flowers bloom
In this funny
Sunny room
I tell us both
A little lie
Before we say goodbye

I'm rooted in illusion
More clear amidst confusion
In a role reversal
With no rehearsal
On the second floor

We lullaby
While lyrics fade
No looking to
The past to grade
What I did
And did not get
Or regret

Never, ever
Quite the same
A family rallies
Round the flame
To soak the warmth

Up to the brim
Before the fires dim

I'm rooted in illusion
More clear amidst confusion
In a role reversal
With no rehearsal
On the second floor

I spend my days
Reeling in rejection
I cover grays
The age of my complexion
But seldom fazed
I've found a new direction

A flight of stairs
A tiled floor
A woman sits
Beyond a door
I fall apart
I just begin
Her laughter let me in
Her laughter let me in
Her laughter let me in

Chapter Three

"My bag is gone!"

After graduating from the LaGuardia High School of Music and Art in Harlem, attending two years at New York University Tisch School of the Arts, and then graduating from an independent study program at State University of New York, I began the quest for a career in the performing arts. I lived on La Guardia Place between Bleeker and Houston, in a studio apartment that I shared with a roommate.

Dad and I found an off-Broadway set designer between shows who was willing to transform this box of a studio into a two-bedroom apartment. Each room was like a ship cabin, but it worked. My roommate worked during the day and I worked at night. So, we both had the place to ourselves for the most part, which is probably how we managed to maintain our friendship and sanity. I had two rules when she first moved in: no overnight guests and no smoking. If you met a boy, you had to go to his place to fool around. She agreed to the rules and loved the large framed poster of Louise Brooks that hung on the fake wall as you walked through the door. For most of the 80s, I tried everything to straighten my out-of-control Flather waves to carry off the Louise Brooks bob. I even went to a hair salon in Chinatown, thinking that they could somehow, magically, transform my fuzz into the black, shiny sheets of hair they sported so elegantly, that always followed orders, even in the worst summer humidity. It never worked, but I tried alright. I have the decade of head shots to prove it.

I worked part time at the Pineapple Dance and Fitness Center, located on the corner of Houston and Broadway. I was the evening receptionist and practiced my newfound customer service skills while standing behind the membership desk. In the 80s the fitness business began to take off, and this old downtown warehouse was transformed into a combination gym and dance studio. The teachers and members were Soho chic with an earthy crunchy twist. They consumed brown rice and tofu lunches while wearing white Capezio dance boots and flowing, colorful Isadora Duncan-like ensembles. They were my safe place to forget my often disappointing street-pounding days.

I attended grueling musical theater auditions by day and began my Pineapple shift at 4 p.m. I remember at the start of each shift hearing a new talk show called *Oprah* sound from the café television downstairs. My boss was a very thin, edgy man who liked to shock this "girl from the sticks" with his devilish humor. He was a retired modern dancer who now ran the dance studio and was a fierce protector of each dancer who entered our doors. I would see young, gorgeous men and women, from time to time, step into his office in tears. His door would shut and we would know not to interrupt the support going on behind the glass. I was the Mary Richards to his Mr. Grant. Instead of letting me go (as any other boss running a business would do), Bill would cover all my shifts and have my job waiting for me if I, miraculously, got cast in an out-of-town musical.

Bill sized up every boy I dated. I would eagerly bring them into the studio, desperately needing his approval. His silence spoke volumes. He would simply look the boys up and down and in the eyes, with a "Pleased to meet you" and then walk away. It drove me nuts. No one was good enough for me! Bill never lied to anyone. He knew the boys I dated were gay. I did not.

When I think of Bill, I think of Joni Mitchell's "Dog Eat Dog," Whitney Houston's "How Will I Know" and just about every note the Eurythmics recorded up until this point. Bill drank espresso coffee, smoked too many cigarettes and didn't eat at all. He had a mischievous look in his eyes and a laugh that suggested a dirty joke. I would count on that laugh to wake up my sleeping audiences when he attended the humble beginnings of my one-woman show career. In the upstairs Cabaret room of the original 55 Grove Street Duplex, Bill would howl at every painful comedic attempt I made. I passed the old Duplex a couple of months ago all boarded up. The Duplex I knew is gone and so is Bill.

When I learned of his death years later, I regretted that I was not more of a friend in return. I was not close enough to him to know the cause of his death. Bill was the kind of person to fight a silent battle. He had no patience for pity, let alone anyone's help. He just left one day and that was that.

Because of Bill, the Pineapple Dance Studio was a safe haven for many young artists trying to spread their wings while paying city rent. This unsung hero made all the difference between a young performer surviving or moving back home, defeated by the tough and competitive apple we call New York. I miss Bill. I miss too many men.

One day during this Pineapple/auditioning chapter, my dear friend Barbara was in town visiting friends and family. After college, Barbara had moved to Atlanta. She was drawn to the lush landscapes surrounding old southern homes. I would savor her handwritten letters that vividly spoke of her days spent painting and her nights spent flirting with "art boys." I loved the image of Barbara sipping cold beers in one of her cotton vintage dresses, while sitting on the railing of one of those sleeping, southern porches she adored.

The day she left New York City to drive to Atlanta, I sent her off with an antique leather jacket. I said, "This way I am right there with you." We cried and hugged tightly as we always do, taking an emotional picture of the other to have for the months that would pass until we would compare life notes again in person. I love to brag about the risks my Barbara takes. Her oil paintings sit on my wall today, serving as markers for each adventure she takes on, full throttle; painter, teacher, wife, mother and Karate black belt, just to name a few.

Barbara and I met in biology class on the first day of the tenth grade. Someone offered me a Wise potato chip. I turned to Barbara who sat behind me and asked if she knew how many calories one chip had. Well, she did. From that moment on we were the other's safe place for all teenage anxieties, highs and lows. At first glance, it didn't look as if we had that much in common. Barbara was cool. She smoked cigarettes, wore a denim jacket with a Rolling Stones patch sewn in, was a competitive tennis player and drove a '67 Nova as soon as she got her license. I didn't smoke, didn't know much about Mick Jagger and to this day, never learned to drive. In that calorie-counting exchange we became life-long sisters, free of apology, judgment or jealousy, strangely understanding the other's passions we knew very little about.

So, Barbara was in town visiting family and friends and we agreed to meet after one of my auditions at a pizza/cappuccino place in Times Square. I had just finished an audition for a musical being performed in Sarasota, Florida, and was asked to come back a couple of hours later. This is called a "callback" audition. We sat as we always do, completely engrossed in the other's stories. So engrossed was I that I did not realize that my gray, canvas bag containing my music, head shots, date book, wallet, keys and cosmetics was being stolen from right under my feet. I learned that day that you always wear your bag while seated in a restaurant or bar. You should literally wear it around your knees, ladies. So, after the initial panic and the fruitless search for the bag, Barbara walked me to Colony Music to buy a piece of sheet music for the callback and loaned me $20 to get to my Pineapple shift on time.

I sat in the callback waiting room with nothing but my "Superstar" sheet music in the Colony Music paper bag. I had no powder or lip gloss to conceal the drama I had just weathered while the ladies seated next to me primped. I remember watching these actresses and assuming that they were much better than me, and began to count myself out of the running. But I didn't leave. I stayed to complete my audition.

When it was my turn to enter the room, I attempted to entertain the gentlemen behind the desk with a humorous take on my ordeal and apologized for only having this one song to sing. They laughed politely at my shtick and seemed impressed with my grit and dedication to attend the audition despite being robbed. I then blasted out "Long ago and oh, so far away. I fell in love with you before the second show...." with a voice sounding in my head, *They don't want you. They don't want you. They don't want you.* I finished the song, collected my sheet music, passed through the waiting room of competitors that I felt were so much better than me, and began to cry alone in the elevator. This was a bad day.

Bill tried to make me laugh. He made some wicked, off-color eating disorder joke about Karen Carpenter because of my "Superstar" song choice that she had made famous. I called my roommate to let her know I would need to be let in that night, and thankfully got lost in my duties answering phones and checking membership cards as dancers passed my desk to take the floor bar class. The phone rang a few hours later.

"Hello, is Meg Flather there?"

"Yes, this is she."

"Hi. I have your bag."

"You are kidding me!"

"No. I work at a soup kitchen for the homeless here in Times Square. Apparently, one of our clients took your bag and the cash and then dumped it in one of our garbage cans. I looked in your date book and saw Pineapple was written in your datebook for today. I looked up the number in the phone book. What is Pineapple?"

"A dance and fitness center."

"Oh, interesting. Anyway, I found you. How wonderful! I will hold your bag until you can come and collect it. When will that be?"

"Oh, right now. Right now. Thank you very much."

Of course, wonderful, wonderful Bill simply said, "Go, go, go. I will cover the desk until you get back."

It was dark as my cab pulled up to a gray city building that instantly made me feel sad. I hesitated to leave the taxi. I had never seen a homeless shelter before, let alone walked through one. The taxi driver volunteered to wait for me while I collected my bag. There are angels on every city corner if you just keep your eyes open for them. I realized that my gray canvas bag had seen a side of NYC that I had never experienced. I felt guilty for my squeaky clean existence and realized I was happy that some homeless person got my $35.

I walked through this shelter as men and women all sat at bare tables eating their colorless dinners on Styrofoam plates. I passed them quickly and forced a smile that tried to say, *I am not judging you.* Finally, I collected my bag in the office and jumped back into my taxi, bound for Pineapple.

When I inspected my bag I was relieved that my wallet with all my ID cards, date book, sheet music and house keys were all there. However, I was overjoyed that my cosmetic bag was completely intact. I remember thinking that was pretty funny. Why do cosmetics mean this much to me? It was only makeup after all.

Felt Like Home

Once there was a valley
Where we used to run
And climb
To smell the favorite flower

Once we lived the story
Once we fed the laughter
Once the cup runeth over

It felt like home
Where there's no need to hide
What I must do
To fill me up inside
Where voices don't distract and lead astray
Where silence is my guide
I think I'll stay, hey

I'm weakened by the hold
Of faceless, distant preaching
A sermon to let go
Of that which I am reaching

What happened to the force
Continually burning
Keeping train on track
To all that I am yearning?

Home
Where there's no need to hide
What I must do
To fill me up inside
Where voices don't distract and lead astray
Where silence is my guide
I think I'll stay

18

If only I could shift
The eyes in which I see
The valley is not gone
It grows inside of me

Help me to return
To that familiar ground
Where last I set my visions
Free

Home
Where there's no need to hide
What I must do
To fill me up inside
Where voices don't distract and lead astray
Where silence is my guide
I think I'll stay

Home
Where there's no need to hide
What I must do
To fill me up inside
Where voices don't distract and lead astray
Where silence is my guide
I think I'll stay, hey

Once there was a valley
Where we used to run
And climb
To smell the favorite flower

Once we lived the story
Once we fed the laughter
Once the cup runneth over

Chapter Four

"I am hoping this is a date."

Boys scared me. I had some questionable interactions with them growing up. While living on the island of Saipan (our last Peace Corps post), I remember the older island boys repeatedly tried to bribe me to pull up my dress in return for Coca Cola and Cracker Jacks. Although I was slightly curious about these boys and tempted because I loved Coca Cola and Cracker Jacks, I always heard an inner alarm sound and knew to run home as fast as I could. I remember how my flip flops filled with sand as I pounded down the dirt road to our house, and how my little cotton dress stuck to my back with nervous perspiration. My parents were off building schools, clinics and training volunteers. I was not brave enough to share these boy stories with the island women that cared for me. So, I kept them inside. I kept them inside for a very long time.

After the Peace Corps, the family settled in Sudbury, Massachusetts. One winter while sledding, an older teenage boy asked if he could join me. Without giving me any time to respond, he hopped on board my sled at the top of a big hill. I didn't feel good. Something was wrong. Why didn't he play with the kids his own age? While my sled was whisking its way to the bottom of the hill, his hand was finding its way down the back of my snowpants. I remember his cold fingers pressed against my scared, sweaty skin. Frozen in time and trapped on this ride, I could not make a sound. What angers me most about this memory is my passivity. Instead of protesting when we reached the bottom of the hill, I silently took the rope handle of my sled and ran home. I kept this one inside as well.

When my friends hosted co-ed parties in high school, I spent most of the evening in the kitchen with their parents. These mothers and fathers quietly knew this Flather girl was not ready for what was going on in the next room and listened so patiently to me as I tried to fill the awkward silence. I would be the last to flirt, kiss and date. It did not help that I studied musical theatre where the straight boys were just a bit cocky for my taste. They knew how in demand they were and I found that unattractive, to say the least. They also were claimed quickly by the precocious girl in the cast. The confident, leggy siren among us would know to hike her leotard up to her hipbones and close the deal long before we all met for the first read through.

So, this slow bloomer waited a long, long time. I was not ready for the steamy meetings in bars, followed by awkward, "You have to go now" mornings that my college friends endured. The subway ride home the next day wearing yesterday's dress, smelling of beer and cigarettes was something I knew I could not hack. So, while others were experimenting with boys, I was thankfully being distracted by a whole new art form, thanks to Christian.

Christian was and is a brilliant singer and pianist. We were both freshman musical theatre majors and I knew he was ahead of his time. Although he was strongly encouraged by our professors to work in the theatre, I believe he was torn because of his phenomenal musical gifts. He could play and sing any type of music from the most authentic place. He never got the "You were indicating" notes from our drama teachers after performing a monologue or scene in class. He kept it real.

Christian heard about this art form called "Cabaret" and learned that if we put a one-hour show together we could audition for a club, charge a cover and perform whatever we wanted. Truth be told, I was his second choice. He had written the piece to perform with another actress in our class, but she dropped out, luckily for me. In time, I came up with our name, "Leather and Flather" because Christian shaved his head, wore leather and I, well…, I was Flather.

We practiced religiously for about a year and when "the act" was ready we first performed it for a circle of close friends in my parent's living room, who lovingly gave it an enthusiastic two thumbs up. So, after this night of safety before family and friends, it was time we attend what they called an open mike. Christian heard of one that took place on Friday nights at Ye Olde Triple Inn.

Christian signed us up as I journeyed alone to 8th Avenue to meet him. We ordered water and sat patiently amidst a crowd of strangers consuming many "spirits" in this beloved Irish pub. The other singers were much older than us, but we stayed and waited our turn nonetheless. When a wave of nerves came over me, I just knew to look to Christian who remained very calm, very serene that night. Our turn finally came. It was the first time I would hear a voice announce, "Ladies and Gentlemen, Leather and Flather!" When Christian began the intro, tinkling the high keys of the piano, as he had the hundreds of times we practiced the medley before, I knew to take a deep breath and give this everything I had. I would also partner, truly partner with another artist for the first time in front of a live audience.

The crowd cheered and cheered. They liked us! They really, really liked us! We agreed that this was the affirmation we needed to schedule an audition for a club that would give us a full hour to perform our show. As we began to pack up and leave Ye Olde Triple Inn, it was Christian who spotted my father, my father, in his signature blue wind breaker and Yankees baseball cap. Dad was seated at the bar the whole time, anonymously witnessing this huge event while allowing us this first free of parental attention, expectation and pressure.

Dad was proud and told us so. He also knew we had not eaten. So, the three of us went for burgers nearby and toasted this first on soda. This story reflects my father's unique, progressive parenting style. If I gave him all the room in the world to surprise me, when he did, it was extraordinary. He would go on to surprise me many times in my career, showing up unannounced, seated in the darkness alongside the other strangers in my audiences.

So, we auditioned for The Duplex, got a full hour slot to perform our full show and pleased yet another audience. From that success, we continued to play many Cabaret clubs. Through "Leather and Flather" I was introduced to the works of artists like Joe Jackson, Rickie Lee Jones, Kate Bush, Joan Armatrading, The Roches, Janis Ian, The Beatles, James Taylor, Joni Mitchell, Howard Jones, obscure jazz and blues standards, and comedic material made famous by Gilda Radner and Carol Burnett

We were the pop, rock Burns and Allen of Cabaret and NYC was so kind to us. We actually were well reviewed in Backstage Magazine and given the first Bistro Award for Best Musical Comedy Act. I know with certainty that Christian saved my creative life, which means he saved my life.

In the spring of 1986, Christian and I knew the currant act (we did many) was a good one and it was time to document it with a video. After my dance class that day I splurged on a short plaid skirt, fishnet stockings, sleeveless black turtleneck, matching huge hoop earrings, and red, red lipstick. I bravely walked in to a West Village hair salon and said to the gentleman, "Do what needs to be done to this!" He gave me a cute, edgy version of my 1920s bob, worked with my waves and curls and told me to embrace what was out of control. I said that I would try. To this day I still try to embrace what is out of control.

Christian and I were pumped up and ready to rock and roll in front of the camera to a sold out audience. My parents were there and I believe Bill with his wonderful laugh was there too. But a new laugh I had not heard before was distractingly wonderful and food for my soul. That laugh belonged to Les.

Les worked with Jeff at a club in Times Square. I must have handed Les a "Leather and Flather" flyer while hoping Jeff would be the one to attend. But Jeff did not come and Les did. In the darkness of The Duplex, Les howled at my comedic attempts and clapped hard after each ballad. Something was happening. When the audience cleared and all the post-show congratulations were over, Les lingered. He asked if I had eaten and if he could take me out? Of course I had not eaten. I never ate! I was happy to stroll to the Caliente Cab Company on the corner of 7th Avenue and Bleeker Street, balancing my many bouquets of flowers in both arms with Les, the perfect gentleman, carrying my bags.

Well, those huge fish bowls of ground ice, salt and Tequila went straight to my head. Every fantasy, hope and heart ache poured out of me. Les was transfixed by my every word. I was not scaring this one away. However, I still regarded Les as Jeff's good friend and Jeff was the one I wanted. I was clueless to the fact that Les liked me. He liked me a lot. Finally, Les leaned across the chips and guacamole with his dark, chocolate, sparkling eyes to say, "Meg, I am hoping this is a date."

That was that. Cupid shot an arrow right through my sleeveless black turtleneck. What a pleasant surprise! What a huge gift on an already perfect night. Les walked me home and in the shadows of a brick building along Bleeker Street, he kissed me. I had a boyfriend. I had a boyfriend just in time for spring.

Kiss With Our Clothes On

Let's take a breath
Let's take a beat
Let's take a stroll
Hold hands on the street
Talk in the present tense
Return to innocence

'Cause we're playing with matches
We're dancing too deep
Up to the edge
Of a cliff that's too steep
Too steep too soon
Lighten up this tune

We can kiss
With our clothes on
Anticipating
We can flirt
Over the phone
While we are waiting
While we are waiting

'Cause there's one
Thing I know
I got the time
To watch this thing grow
Bit by bit
Day by day
Rewind to hear it play

So let's take a breath
Let's take a beat
Let's take a stroll
Hold hands on the street
Talk in the present tense

Return to innocence

We can kiss
With our clothes on
Anticipating
We can flirt
Over the phone
While we are waiting
While we are waiting

'Cause we both know where
This thing could wind up
'Cause we both have tasted
From the sacred cup
But the wine's gone right
To my head
And it's my heart that must be led

We can kiss
With our clothes on
Anticipating
We can flirt
Over the phone
While we are waiting

We can kiss
With our clothes on
Anticipating
We can flirt
Over the phone
While we are waiting
While we are waiting

Chapter Five

"Well, she's not much of a singer."

Les called me the next morning (the next morning!) to assure me that what I thought had taken place actually took place and that his courtship wishes and kiss were sincere. Exhale. Huge sigh of relief. He then insisted on taking me to dinner that night (that night!) and told me he would pick me up at my apartment at 7 p.m. sharp. No game playing here.

Les was a serious dancer, acrobat and aspiring choreographer and was soon to be rewarded with much out of town work. After the positive reviews, the award and the success of our videotaped night at The Duplex, Christian lovingly threw me out of the nest, insisting I fly solo and perform my first one-woman show that summer. But a few weeks previously, I had had a callback audition to also play the role of Luisa, Guido's devoted, neglected wife in a production of the musical, *Nine*, which was being performed in a theatre in Connecticut.

The callback audition was in a building on the corner of Broadway and 56th Street that was an old hotel turned apartment building. I entered one of those apartments where the choreographer, director and theatre producers sat in sofas and chairs by a fireplace. There was little room for me and the grand piano, let alone the "fourth wall" we actors were trained to depend upon. But I began. I sang "My husband makes movies. To make them he lives a kind of dream."

My melancholy, hopefulness understood the character's dilemma. I knew what it was to protect someone who disappoints you, always making those disappointments OK to the outside world. So, instead of "acting" the piece, I tried to simply be and tell the story as honestly as I could. Well, after

I finished, I thought for certain that I had had a performance breakthrough of sorts, right there by the fireplace. I assumed those in the room felt the same way, so what did I do next? After completing my audition, I made the huge, huge, HUGE mistake of listening through the door outside in the hall to hear what they had to say about me inside. What did I hear? I heard the director say, "Well, she's not much of a singer, is she?"

Oh, no, no, no! Stupid, stupid, stupid! Why did you do that, Meg? Why did you listen?

Over an over, I berated myself while my heart raced and felt like it weighed a thousand pounds. I rode the gray elevator to the dingy lobby and thank God I had somewhere to go. Thank God I had my Pineapple shift starting at 4 p.m. and Bill to say something wicked about all directors. All directors!

So, I had written the whole *Nine* thing off, to say the least, but while waiting for Les to pick me up for our date, my phone rang.

"Hello?"

"Hello, is Meg Flather there?"

"This is she."

"Hi, Meg. I am calling to offer you the lead role of Luisa in the production of *Nine* that you auditioned for a few weeks ago."

"Really? Are you sure?" (*Lord, how Meg is that? Can't I play it cool for once in my life?*)

So, I got the job. After that horror show of a callback experience, I got the part and had to prepare myself to work with the director who thought I wasn't "much of a singer." Right after I hung up the phone Les arrived. When I told him of my good news he cheered. I had never experienced anyone believing in me the way Les did that summer.

Les used to make homemade cards for me covered with sparkling dust. With colorful markers he wrote, "Soar! Soar, Meg, soar!" in big, bold letters. Oh, how I wanted to soar for Les. I wanted him to be so proud of me. But even on my brighter days, I felt darker than Les. His Cancerian sensitivity was mixed with leprechaun magic. He was not quite mortal. He danced in streets and up and down staircases with no inhibitions. It is only now that I comprehend how much his childlike innocence and paradoxical "Why not you?" old soul was trying to teach me. I was so lucky, so lucky to bask in Les.

So, we had a wonderful summer. Les was cast in a production of *Kismet* in Toronto and I performed *Nine* in Connecticut with his picture in my wallet.

After my solo venture at The Duplex, with a beaming Christian seated in the audience, I traveled to Canada to see Les thrive. He saved up all his money to meet me at the airport in a stretch limousine complete with champagne. He treated me like a queen and showed me off to all cast members. But behind closed doors, he put a stop to anything more than a kiss just in time.

By the time *Kismet* closed, it was fall and Les began to drift. His dark chocolate eyes were suddenly hesitant and slightly sad. He finally encouraged me to see other people after he was cast in a national tour. I guess he broke up with me, but he was so beautifully unconventional that it wasn't that clear.

From the road he sent me cards and his itinerary. He took my long distance, lonely calls and I counted on his, "Soar, Meg, soar" pep talks. But during that tour Les finally let himself love a man. He had been experimenting for years; back, forth, man, woman, yes, no. It was exhausting for Les. Although my heart was broken, I was relieved for him. I knew that I really loved him when his happiness trumped the needs of my broken heart and bruised ego.

On one of his trips home, we walked through Central Park. I told him that I was so happy for him and that he deserved a deep, loving and lasting relationship out in the light. He was silent as I spoke, probably a little uncomfortable, but I like to think I helped him begin to accept himself. I feared that his conservative roots did not help him "soar" in this department.

Les died of AIDS years later. I was told that when his parents and his partner were both in his hospital room at the same time, all the machines monitoring his body functions went haywire. When either his parents or his partner left the room, the machines quieted down. I hated hearing this. I wanted my Les to love and lust freely, just as he danced down city streets and up and down stairwells that summer we shared. I remembered my Les always uninhibited, even with all eyes watching him, watching him always in awe.

I spoke at his Peter Pan-like memorial service. I told the congregation of performers and family about how he taught me to soar. I looked up and said, "Oh, dear Les, I will try to soar. But I know one thing for sure, you are soaring now, my dear friend. You are soaring now."

To this day, I think I see Les. I will be walking my city streets with something ridiculously silly bothering me. Then in an instant, a vibrant, fit and flying brunette energy will whisk by, determined to interrupt my inner rant. It is Les. It is always Cancerian Les, determined to lighten up my triple Aquarian self with his neverending lesson on how to soar. Thank you, my Les.

I Will Wait With You

They will wait for you
On the other side
Of a distant bridge
When the worst is over

But I will wait with you
While the storm blows through
And take you by the hand
And lead you to the clover

You say that no one's there to care
They stop to whisper
Or to stare
But not me
This very moment you're lovely

Upstream you thrust and dive
It shows how you're alive
What you're made of
And it measures my love

So we'll just persevere
'Til the grey skies clear
In your boat at sea
Darling, just you and me

They will wait for you
On the other side
Of a distant bridge
When the worst is over

But I will wait with you
While the storm blows through
And take you by the hand
And lead you to the clover

Chapter Six

Another *click, click, click*

I heard sandals *click, click, click* and bracelets *jingle, jingle, jingle* outside my dorm room door. This percussive duet was followed by the muffled tones of a pay phone conversation. It was Carolyn who was cast as Guido's mother in that same production of *Nine*. I didn't know her well at this point. I was a bit of a loner.

While other cast members socialized and savored the nights off before the show opened, I went back to my vocal silence and humidifier. I was precious in those days, thinking my instrument was somehow broken, less than, that I was a fraud. I was still haunted by the "She's not much of a singer" comment that had sounded through the audition callback door. I would wake up early to complete my taped dance and voice class exercises, knowing full well that we would be thoroughly warmed up as a cast a few hours later. I would reward this deprivation with a carefully rationed cup of cottage cheese and a chopped apple.

I was twenty two years old, with little experience with men, and little to no understanding of the mystery called marriage. So, how did I know something was amiss in Carolyn's voice? More importantly, how did I know to put a note under her door that read, "Whatever it is, it will be OK." It was one of those channeling moments where something bigger and wiser than me was speaking from within and was "spot on" about a total stranger. I just knew Carolyn was unhappy in her marriage and needed a safe place to share.

She discovered the note and knocked on my door. Her brilliant blue eyes seemed to be silently asking *Who are you?* while she held the note neatly folded between her perfectly manicured fingers. From that moment in the doorway, Carolyn began to challenge my addiction to deprivation as I gave the humidifier and vocal silence a rest that night. Already I was in debt to this surrogate mother, surrogate daughter, and everything in between.

There was an age difference between us and to this day I don't know what that difference is. It doesn't matter. It has nothing to do with our sisterhood that we both believe has walked through lifetimes together.

It was a pivotal summer for me. I ultimately earned positive reviews in *Nine*. The "She's not much of a singer" director turned out to be a raging alcoholic and was fired during rehearsals. Annette, the choreographer, was promoted to director and demanded that I give the role and win to myself. When I listened through that callback audition door weeks prior to our working together, Annette had said, "I like her." It's funny how we focus on the negative comment when other supportive voices are trying to reach out and encourage us. Like Les, Annette had dark chocolate eyes and in her own way, challenged me to soar. It takes a village, and my village was abundant that summer of '86.

Years later, when I was lacking faith, Carolyn bought me a rosary and taught me the Hail Mary. She made it clear that I did not have to be a Catholic or even religious to gain the inner peace that she experienced when having one of her "chats" with Mary. I was amazed that I shared her experience that very night. The maternal support I felt while reciting the prayer over and over again, was a welcome gift that I did not realize I craved. The idea of Mary cradling me in her powder blue cloak inspired me to write the song, "Powder Blue." When I sing the song, a powerful mixture of Mary and Carolyn's love comes to my mind. This truly is a miracle when you consider that my perfect Sunday morning ritual is watching *Meet The Press*, not attending church.

Powder Blue

When the waves within grow restless
And no compass guides me through
I turn to you, my Mary
You are the color, powder blue

When the roads I travel fail me
I look up to your skies
I feel your grace
Your embrace
The fog then washes from my eyes

And when I don't believe
Not ready to receive
You wait
While so serene
My most forgiving
Holy Queen
My most forgiving
Holy Queen

You are my deepest breath
That whispers "I am strong"
Sun rising after tranquil rest
My melody
My finest song

Little winks that come from heaven
Remind me I'm on track
They gently push me from behind
And never let me fall far back

And when I don't believe
Not ready to receive
You wait
While so serene

My most forgiving
Holy Queen
My most forgiving
Holy Queen

Trusting, falling
Through your branches
I always feel you
Catching me
Your roots grow in the earth
Mother Mary
Giving tree
Mother Mary
Giving tree

Oh, Silent Night
I feel you there
Like timeless embers keeping warm
You are the smell of ocean air
After a necessary storm

And when I don't believe
Not ready to receive
You wait
While so serene
My most forgiving
Holy Queen

And when I don't believe
Not ready to receive
You wait
While so serene
My most forgiving
Holy Queen
My most forgiving
Holy Queen

Chapter Seven

"We love you, Mugga!"

Many young performers are inherently insecure and think that whatever they have to offer is not quite enough. Some deal with these incorrect assumptions by imitating famous people. I know I did. For most of my Summer Stock experience I did all I could to sound like Julie Andrews. (Oh, that went well. Not!)

Then through Cabaret I began to understand that the artists I admired became successful because they had the courage to share themselves and their instruments honestly. Thankfully, over time, the combination of insightful directors and Christian's outrageous Cabaret material began to draw my essence out to play when I wasn't looking. I began to hear the audience reward these raw moments with approving applause and cheers. One rewarding cheer that cut through all the rest, was the distinct and glorious sound of Jewels shrieking, "We love you, Mugga!" Jewels was my colorful friend who was responsible for the risks I took and the fun I had.

Jewels and I met after auditioning for the musical theatre track at NYU. On Mondays, Wednesdays, and Fridays our group of about 16 students would take the A train to Port Authority, walk west to 10th Avenue, and study speech, sense memory, voice, jazz, ballet, acting technique, and scene study. This all took place in the small walk-up, Off-Broadway theatre called The Actor's and Director's Lab. The building still stands today on what is now called Theatre Row.

Jewels was a petite pistol of energy, enthusiasm and street smarts, and a Gemini, like both Mom and Dad. She had a huge heart and an endless capacity for joy. Jewels was always up for breakfast, lunch, dinner, a movie, a play, a concert, a party, or a shopping spree. She never missed a friend's performance. When we met at the age of 18, she was a member of all the acting unions, had been in a Broadway musical and was to be cast in a Robert Deniro film the following winter. She was making a lucrative living performing voice-overs in national radio and television commercials, and yet she was the one to recognize me after the audition.

"I know you! You played Jesus!"

In my senior year in high school I played Jesus in *Godspell*. My visionary teacher decided this tall girl with bangs and a space between her two front teeth would play the Holy One. When word spread throughout the city public school system, there was much commotion, to say the least.

So, I was thankful for Jewels' recognition that NYU audition day. I was feeling pretty disconnected from the gifts of confidence that *Godspell* and high school in general had left behind. For a brief moment, her "I know you" pulled me back from the abyss of freshman year insecurity and my father's wise words began to sound again in my head. "You always hold your own, Margaret. Why would this time be any different?"

Jewels was precocious. She grew up in NYC and seemed to own the subways, parks, theatres, cafes and clubs. She also knew how to talk to boys. I was quite the opposite, spending my college nights alone with my trusted vocal rest and humidifier.

On our first day of classes at the Actor's and Director's Lab, the dean shared one of his private rituals with us. He said that when he was overwhelmed by fears of theatrical unemployment, he would go to the country and stand beneath a night sky of sparkling stars. He would witness that the stars "up there" were not crowded, so why wouldn't it be the same case down here? There was plenty of room for all of us to shine.

Jewels understood this. Jewels lived this. She thrived on her friends' successes. She soaked in our wins and then used those wins to fuel her next day, class or project. When we shopped, she chose accessories that flattered me. When I wasn't ready for clubs of boys, she brought white wine coolers to my fire escape, and every encore I performed was met with a "We love you, Mugga!"

During this pivotal chapter, Jewels was essential to my confidence to plan yet another show. We would meet at Le Figaro Café on Macdougal Street after her morning voice-over bookings. I would drink my coffee with steamed milk and eat my cottage cheese with apples. She would listen and listen and listen to all my creative and personal wins and disappointments. Oh, and Jewels made me laugh. When I was a little too analytical, or intensely trying to control something uncontrollable, she would gently smile, tilt her head to the side and lovingly say, "Oh, Meg." When Christian witnessed one of our, "Oh, Meg" exchanges, he insisted that I call one of my favorite shows, *Oh Meg!* Needless to say Jewels attended that show and cheered with even more enthusiasm than usual, knowing she played a key role in the inception of it all.

Jewels understood something about self-acceptance and acceptance of others. She knew the strengths and limits of each friend and was rarely disappointed in anyone. She didn't compare herself to others personally or professionally and I always felt safe to succeed. With Jewels, I never feared that passive aggressive response of envy which is often associated with performing peers.

This city angel sported pink, frosted Revlon lipstick, a halo of black curls and instead of wings, flew about NYC in a collection of vintage Hawaiian shirts with matching, sunglasses. Heaven and just about every one of my Cabaret audiences never looked so good.

Don't Listen to the Fear

It finds you alone with a question
Where no loved one can rescue
When faced with a fork in the roadway
Where no angel can lead you

What was the wish it took over?
What visions were set?
It sounded so wise, so much older
Somehow it made you forget

Don't listen to the logic
So practical and clear
Don't listen to the fear

Just when detecting its traces
Alarmed by the size and the shape
It will change place with a beautiful face
It will succeed to escape

You may agree with its listed demands
Read with a comforting tone
But don't surrender
You'll die in familiar
Gamble to fly with unknown

Don't listen to the logic
So practical and clear
Don't listen to the fear
Don't listen to the fear

It hides in a gesture
Behind nervous laughter
Disguised as a mother's whisper
Don't listen to

Don't step on the crack
You'll break your mama's back
Don't step on the crack
You'll break your mama's back
Don't step on the crack
You'll break your mama's back
Don't step on the crack
You'll break your mama's

It finds you alone with a question
Where no loved one can rescue
When faced with a fork in the roadway
Where no angel can lead you

Don't listen to the logic
So practical and clear
Don't listen to the fear
Don't listen to the fear
Don't listen to the fear
Don't listen to the fear
Don't listen to the fear

Chapter Eight

"My bag is gone!" Again!

I had inherited a bit of my father's restless spirit in regards to work and money. Shaking up how I paid my rent felt like buying new school supplies with Mom. Standing in the aisles of the Sudbury Star Market selecting my new lunch box and book bag was evidence that an exciting new adventure was about to begin, or at least a new crush. Finding a new survival job felt exactly the same way. It was now 1987, and I was getting antsy working at Pineapple.

I went to an audition for a show being cast in Greenwich Village and like most audition experiences, the gift was making a new friend. I met Bebe at this audition. We were both dreading the dance part of the audition because we were "singers who dance," rather than "dancers who sing." We got to talking and she told me that she worked for a chiropractor who treated most of the Broadway community, including the casts of *Cats* and *Les Miserables*. They had just lost their receptionist and would I be interested? My celebrity worship was in full gear. She had me with *Cats*.

"You bet! When do I start?"

Pineapple was warm and generous when the time came and I finished my final shift. They left the door wide open if things with the chiropractor didn't work out. But like leaving home, I had to venture into this new territory. The chiropractic practice was a converted three bedroom apartment, located in a tall, doorman building on West 53rd Street. Jerry and Elaine Orbach lived in this building, and the street is now called Jerry Orbach Way. Each morning I walked to West 4th Street and took the local 8th Avenue train to the 50th Street stop. I sang show tunes with Bebe all day, answered the phone, made and cancelled patient appointments, collected payments and cleaned the bathrooms.

Auditioning for theatre jobs was growing old. I had done two productions of *Nine* at this point, playing the same role opposite the same Guido twice. My heart belonged to Cabaret, and I no longer needed my afternoons free to attend theatrical auditions. I just needed to cover my monthly bills and schedule my weekly voice classes, rehearsals and Cabaret acts around the hours of this practice. I remember how freeing it was to chat with *Cats* and *Les Miserables* cast members as they waited to be adjusted before their half hour matinee call time. I felt no envy. I was a singer, a musician, an artist now! They were very patient with me as I made this point painfully clear while handing them my next show flyer tucked into their payment receipts.

About a year later, the chiropractor offered me two free tickets to see *The Phantom of the Opera* that she could not use. One of her patients sold theatre tickets for a living and dropped them off as a thank you gift for the effective treatment he had received for his lower back pain. However, days before the performance, she told me that she had lost the tickets and was very sorry.

Being the crafty gal that I am, I called the patient, and he left word with the box office to let me in and to escort my friend and me to where we would have been seated if we still had the tickets. Indeed, I am crafty and a bit of a secret agent. I always could sniff out where Mom had hidden my Christmas and birthday gifts. Months before the celebrations would occur, I would have already seen the doll, book, album, new outfit or accessory. My performances opening these gifts on Christmas mornings and birthdays deserved at least a Golden Globe, let alone an Oscar! This "sniffing out the goods" gift has come in handy over the years, to say the least.

Back to *Phantom*, my friend and I were sitting happily in our orchestra seats waiting for the show to begin when the male employee of the chiropractic practice showed up with my tickets.

"The doctor gave these to me yesterday."

Yuck. How could a healer be such a liar? My friend and I were humiliated as we left our orchestra seats to stand and watch the show from the back. I was now in no mood to enjoy the show. The larger-than-life chandelier flying over the orchestra section that I was no longer sitting in did nothing whatsoever for me. My boss had lied to me and I needed to make another change.

The universe always responds to requests. You just have to be patient and stay alert to recognize the answer you get. Weeks later I was having lunch on Prince Street. The Mary Poppins carpet bag was the rage and I had one, but I had not learned the lesson years earlier of wearing my hand bag while eating in a restaurant. When it was time to pay the bill, my Mary Poppins carpet bag was gone, and this time it was not returned to me.

My wallet, check book, date book, sunglasses, keys, and my cosmetic bag were gone as well. I called Mom in tears, and she offered to meet me the next day to purchase a new bag and replacement makeup.

"But I am not buying you another one of those ridiculous carpet bags, Meg!"

The next day was a Sunday. Mom and I first went to the bag department to buy a new shoulder bag. Then we arrived at my favorite cosmetic counter. This was a life-changing moment in many ways. The lovely representative stood on one side of the counter in a crisp, white lab coat, with her brilliant red hair neatly coiffed, impeccable nails, and a clean and lady-like application of makeup on a flawless, porcelain complexion. She was completely focused on my needs. Even though I had had a dramatic twenty-four hours prior to this exchange, she neutralized my anxiety and created a warm, comforting and festive energy around Mom and me. She did this while selling us products. She was good, but ironically, she did not have to sell me much. I was prepared for this transaction with my list.

"I need the Quick Corrector in light, Plum Blush, Glossy Black Mascara, Currant Stain Lipstick and that shadow trio, the one that has brown, pink and blue shades in it. You know the one?"

Well, of course she knew the one. She brought Mom and me the testers, and while I was explaining to Mom how all these items worked together and why I needed her to purchase all of them for me right then and there, the lovely lady said, "You know, you really ought to be doing this."

"Doing what?"

"You should be selling cosmetics for us. I can see you have such passion."

That was the moment. I had never dreamed that I could sell cosmetics. I had always thought that these glamorous ladies behind the glass, chrome and Formica counter tops were manufactured in New Jersey along with the bottles of clear toners and yellow moisturizers made famous by the brand. I had never dreamed I could be one of them.

But she was right. I was passionate about this. I had been playing with makeup and skin care since my earliest Christmas memory. Let me correct that. I had been obsessed with makeup and skin care since my earliest Christmas memory.

My Aunt Fiona was my mother's best friend in high school and ended up marrying my mother's older brother, Harry. Fiona was very sophisticated and had a great sense of style. She was and is to this day fiercely loyal to my mother. When she noticed my mother neglecting herself, she would demand that they go shopping in Boston together and that meant going to Saks Fifth Avenue and Lord and Taylor.

Mom would come home with shopping bags of new clothes to hang up in my parent's closet. Mom would be in such a good mood. I would sit on her closet floor as she gently placed a new skirt, blouse, or dress with tags upon a hanger. I would smell the different perfume samplings coming from her wrists and hear about how they ate a delicious lunch right there in the department store.

Fiona understood Mom's capacity for deprivation and was the single friend who knew how to remedy it. She knew that Mom became anxious and overwhelmed when pressured by another to give to herself. It had to be Mom's idea to indulge. It is the difference between someone silently placing a delicious dessert in front of you and allowing you to choose to take a bite and someone demanding you take a bite right now. Fiona understood how to get Mom to pamper herself. I felt so full and complete when witnessing the evidence of these needed feedings. Mom looked so pretty, as many of these outings included a make-over as well. I would be consumed with cosmetic curiosity as new powders, lipsticks, and skin care products were lined up on Mom's bathroom cabinet shelves. Fiona shares my February 14th birthday, and I loved thinking that that meant I also had the potential for such style, fashion sense, and a capacity for such abundance myself one day.

So, Aunt Fiona or Fifi as I called her, bought me "big girl" makeup one year for Christmas, not "little girl" makeup, but Cover Girl, Maybelline and Max Factor. I was so filled with euphoria that I practically rolled around in each of those plastic compacts of shadows, blushes and powders, right there under the overly-decorated Flather Christmas tree.

This makeup collection grew every Christmas, and with it adult cosmetic travel bags to store my colorful treasures in. I would pull these bags out daily to makeup my friends in the neighborhood. I even produced back deck musicals just to apply the makeup on someone, anyone.

Mom and Dad would be at work. Lisa would be studying in her room. Roger would be practicing drums in his room. Julie would be drawing in her room. I would snoop around Dad's desk until I found his carbon paper to compose four invitations to a page which meant eight invitations with the carbon paper. I loved carbon paper. I then would go door to door inviting neighbors for the show that was to be performed on my parents' back deck later that day. The tickets I made from even more carbon paper cost five cents and included popcorn and instant lemonade. I would cast my younger friend, Hanna in the lead role which meant she played the princess or the movie star. I played all the other roles.

As I write this, I realize that not much has changed over the years. I still make flyers, invite people to shows and play all the other roles. When handing out flyers today I often say, "Just call me Flyer Flather! I swear I came out of my mother with a flyer that read, 'It's a girl!'"

I wrote my first song for these backyard productions and no matter how the plot changed from show to show, Hanna sang the same song. Thankfully, my neighborhood audience did not seem to notice or mind.

We would use Mom and Dad's bedroom as our backstage, Mom and Dad's closet as our dressing room, and Mom's clothes mixed with my dress up clothes as our costumes. Mom would pull into the driveway after a long day at the hospital to find all the neighborhood mothers gathered by her back deck and most probably say out loud to herself in the car, "Oh, Meg, no!"

After Mom got over the initial shock of seeing the state of her bedroom, closet and kitchen, she seemed to come alive and enjoy my back deck extravaganzas. These fifteen minute productions created community in our small suburban neighborhood and were often the only opportunity Mom had to talk to the other mothers. She was always driving a little too fast in the opposite direction, racing to keep up with an impossible schedule. I also think she was proud of my moxy as she witnessed these seeds of my future entrepreneurial lifestyle grow.

A few years ago a co-worker shared an observation with me after she attended one of my shows for the first time. She said that it didn't matter if I was answering phones, selling moisturizers or singing songs on a stage. I needed to connect with others and I should do that in a number of ways. She said that all my "hats" were useful and not a mistake. That I should stop apologizing for and embrace the "hat rack" called my career. So, I began to do this. My "hat rack" wasn't going anywhere!

So, back to my life-changing moment, after all the new cosmetics were placed in my new purse, the lovely lady gave me the business card of a woman named Violet. She told me to call her for work. Apparently the company had created a new position called Associate Consultant, which was a part-time, freelance position for employees who required schedule flexibility in order to study, work another job, or raise a family. When I got home that night, I left a message for Violet, soon to be another angel in my NYC story.

What to wear for this job interview? I didn't own a suit or appropriate shoes. I was "artsy" to put it mildly. I did my best with an antique, 1940's black and red silken house dress and my Cabaret red, red, red lipstick. Back in the day, wearing antique house dresses from the Antique Boutique on Broadway was all the rage. It was downright "cool" to do so at both LaGuardia High School of Music and Art and NYU. To really pull the look off, you wore white, flat Capezio jazz dance slippers, funky sun glass frames and carried a Le Sport Sac nylon bag. I didn't look corporate, but I appeared eager and enthusiastic when I met Violet for the first time.

Violet lived in Soho, was a natural beauty and very stylish. Her porcelain Chinese skin, sparkling eyes, perfectly lined red lips, designer suits, and Robert Lee Morris jewelry were a sight to behold. And she mastered that bob hairstyle I was trying to sport for most of the 1980s.

Violet glowed with excitement as I told her my story. She was thrilled to interview me. Me? What did she see in me? I didn't have the experience, training or the wardrobe to compete in the corporate and often political world of cosmetics, but Violet wasn't worried. She gave me the job right then and there, and in a flash my whole life changed. This was not to be another flaky job to make some cash while trying to get famous. This was a career move, although I didn't realize it yet.

Violet said that I would first go for training for two full days at the exclusive hotel, The Essex House. So, wearing my brand new polyester lab coat, I took the R train to 5th Avenue to arrive bright and early for my first day of selling school.

First they fed us a huge breakfast (which I regrettably didn't eat), wanting all new associates to meet each other before class began. What a sight to behold! We were black, white, Jewish, Catholic, Muslim, Hispanic, Asian, gay, straight, right out of high school, middle-aged and seniors. We weren't glamorous, experienced or sophisticated. We had a hunger to learn, to belong and work very, very hard. The company had a gift of recognizing that "special something" beneath the surface in a new hire and went to great lengths and expense to develop it.

When you travel the world, no matter what counter you visit, all associates working for the brand will have had the same training, will follow the same strict counter rules, memorize the same product knowledge and in just about every language imaginable, will recite the same points of difference with pride and gusto, in a perfectly pressed lab coat.

After our breakfast meet and greet, class began. Beverly was our trainer. She was a tall, handsome woman with a passion for educating and empowering women. She taught us how to determine skin type, explained exfoliation (the removal of dull, dead skin cells, which clog and challenge both dry and oily skin) and taught us how to ask open-ended questions to build and close a sale.

When you teach a young woman how to close a sale, you teach her the world.

I have seen over the last few decades of my life that it was this training that provided me with the tools and courage to take care of myself, especially when making phone calls to strangers. You know those 1-800 calls you make to customer service when the service you are paying for is lacking or non-existent? Or those calls you make when overcharged, or if there is a mysterious fee on your bill? Or those calls you make when applying for a job, an apartment, a loan, checking on a health insurance claim, calling an agent you want to represent you, or a club you want to perform in? Beverly taught me how to make those calls.

Beverly helped me put the little girl aside and engage in the world with confidence. She helped grow the assertiveness that I sorely lacked through determining a customer's skin type. She made me want to raise my hand at school and then go back to the counter and apply all I had learned with passion. It was more than selling, it was more than pleasing employers, and it was more than paying my bills. Beverly made me feel powerful and useful when not on a stage.

Women would soon stand in front of my station and trust me with their faces. Younger co-workers would watch how I sold and congratulate me as I waved a happy customer away with a shopping bag loaded with bottles and boxes. This was important for me. I did not have to plan a show, hand out a flyer, or suffer through another theatrical rejection to find purpose. I did not have to apologize at family reunions for the latest "survival job" that was not a Broadway show. The seeds of feeling "enough" as Meg were planted by this new city angel dressed in white.

Thank you, Beverly for the passion. Thank you, Violet, for seeing something beneath the vintage house dress that was worth investing in. I have worked for eleven cosmetic brands since my time with the company. It is Beverly's training that I tap to meet all professional demands and sales goals to this very day.

I graduated from selling school and was to float wherever an Associate Consultant was needed. Each week my schedule and destination would change. I stood behind every New York counter the brand had at the time and that meant eight accounts! We Associate Consultants were trained to arrive wearing our lab coats, black tights and matching, sensible shoes. We all wore silver stud earrings and styled our hair neatly to frame our freshly exfoliated faces.

We were supposed to be examples and energetic shots of enthusiasm to recharge the full time counter staff, who could not help but lose some of the daily "rah-rah" required of them by corporate. We were created to be a freelance team of spare hands to meet the needs of an increased customer base during the gift events. When a customer spent a certain amount of money, she received a gift, and boy, did the ladies show up for this! Herds and herds of women would stand for hours in line, held in place by the same velvet ropes used at rock concerts and movie theatres to maintain order. These events were so huge, they were often reported in the evening news.

The Associate Consultants were the part-timers who exchanged the stability of a steady, full-time schedule, health benefits, paid sick days and vacations, for flexibility to pursue outside passions. We were actors, dancers, musicians, photographers, academics, and some of us spoke English as a second language. We were also working or expecting mothers, and in some cases, grandmothers. Sometimes we were men.

Each counter gave me a community. Women of all backgrounds, ages, levels of education, and reasons for working for the company, stood alongside me. They welcomed me into the fold and became examples as mothers, daughters, sisters, and friends.

There were the young representatives who would stroll into work in the nick of time, just before the starting bell. They were at times hungover, heartbroken, disheveled, wearing stained and wrinkled lab coats that journeyed to work balled up in the bottom of a faded and tired back pack.

Then there were the older ones.

These women taught me some powerful life lessons. They would endure long subway commutes to arrive at the counter long before the starting bell. They were always ready for an unannounced inspection, and their starched lab coats, shoes, tights, earrings, hair, and makeup reflected the strict employee manual. In the darkness of an empty store, they would wipe down their portion of the counter, stock their shelves and count their register drawers. They rarely took breaks, let alone lunch.

We knew not to talk to them. They were there to work, but on snowy or rainy days, or following the holiday season rush, we could talk to them. I would interview them and learn that they were supporting husbands, children, and in some cases, entire family trees "back home" on the same salaries we youngsters complained about and could not make last. Through a silent, stoic work ethic and with admirable consistency, these women twice my age stood to sell cosmetics for over eight hours with gratitude and spirit. Through sheer grit, they taught me more about love and commitment than any show tune, movie or classic novel.

I had mentors too. These women taught me how to walk, talk, dress, shop, and carry myself in a business meeting.

"You never mix your alloys, Meg, never! Use silver or gold, Meg, but never both. And your shoes, belt, hand bag, watch band and glasses must match as well. Wear black or brown, but never both at once." You didn't have to spend money on expensive clothes and accessories to look stylish. You simply had to follow these rules.

My managers went out of their way to develop and promote me. This was a first for me and I was hooked. I increased sales for them and they served as my finishing school. They would also let me take time off if my next Cabaret act required particular focus, making certain that my job was waiting for me once the show closed. But with each departure, I began to see that I missed sales and working in a group. I was helping women for the first time in my life. It was not about my face, my voice, whether I had talent, or whether a boy liked me. I experienced a new freedom by focusing outward. It was not about me at all. What a relief! Finally, I took them up on their offer to promote me to Counter Manager.

The story goes that I was deep in a consultation at the largest counter on the West Side. They were short staffed for a season, so I was posted there as a part-timer until they hired a permanent employee. Instead of the intense freelance existence as an Associate Consultant, always selling during a gift event, I got to experience the day-to-day life behind the counter. This gave me more opportunities to hone my customer service and sales skills. When a shopper strolled to the counter to browse our lipstick towers, I knew just how to ask those open-ended questions to get that shopper in the chair! (Thank you,

Beverly!) Little did I know that while this was going on one night, I was being observed by Donna, Director of Regional Sales.

After work, Donna would stroll along the various accounts incognito to see what life at the counter was like. The night when she spied on me, there I was closing a large sale. What I didn't know was that my co-workers were watching me and according to Donna, learning from me. This meant that I had management potential and that I must be promoted. I was oblivious to all of this.

Kristine, the Account Executive for the largest chain of stores telephoned me after Donna had told her about me. We were to meet for breakfast the next day, but I was torn. I loved being a freelance superstar on my terms, and I loved sailing in for my six hour shift, full of vigor, to be cheered and adored. Was I full-time material? Was I management material? Was I corporate material? I loved Violet, and I loved her team of arty freelancers. I would miss hearing about their various projects when stores were slow—their dance pieces, thesis papers, photography exhibits, and Shakespeare scene study classes.

Ironically, the store I was to work in had just launched a whole new advertising campaign, calling the main floor, "Bway." I was finally going to make it on Broadway, sort of. Life has a sense of humor at times.

Tired of Waiting

Wait for the alarm
Waiting to awake
Waiting to go back to sleep
How much more to take?

Waiting for the bus
Waiting in the rain
Waiting for a lift
Or a pill to stop the pain

Tired of waiting
Are you waiting too?
Tired of waiting
Let's think of something to do
While we are waiting
I could be waiting for you

Waiting to be chosen
To be noticed
Like the best
Waiting in a line
Like lambs to slaughter
Like the rest

Waiting for a change
Something happen
Something new
OK, another Cabernet
Killing time will do

Tired of waiting
Are you waiting too?
Tired of waiting
Let's think of something to do
While we are waiting

I could be waiting for you

Waiting for the changes to take
Always paying for a point of view
Should I settle for the feelings that I fake
'Stead of waiting for the blessed breakthrough?

Waiting for a life
Waiting for a love
Waiting for the final breath
Join the one above

Wait for the alarm
Waiting to awake
Waiting to go back to sleep
How much more to take?

Tired of waiting
Are you waiting too?
Tired of waiting
Let's think of something to do
While we are waiting
I could be waiting for you
I could be waiting for you
I could be waiting for you

Tired of waiting
Tired of waiting
Tired of waiting
Tired of waiting
Tired of waiting
Tired of waiting

Chapter Nine

But was I Counter Manager material?

Kristine's dark, red finger nails performed a new *click, click, click* in my life. When I asked how much I would earn the answer was confusing. I would make an hourly rate less than my freelance rate, but there would be health care benefits, paid holidays, sick days, and vacation days now. There would also be a commission check each month based on what I individually sold and on what my counter sold.

When the clicking began, so did the guessing. Assuming I would meet all these sales goals, I would then make, "This much, Meg," Kristine said as she handed me her calculator with a handsome number flashing upon the screen. But would I meet these goals? If I didn't, how much would I make? I failed to ask this question in the interview.

There were a few other tasks to be performed with this promotion. In addition to managing a team of about seven women on this third floor outpost counter, right off the escalator, I would have to do the count each month. This meant that I would have to count each product at the counter and in the stock room, manually. Then I would fill out a report that Kristine would use to sell more products to the store's beauty buying team. But who said I could count?

Kristine could count.

Kristine began working behind the counters of suburbia as a teenager, and through blood, sweat, and street smarts was promoted to this coveted position. She was a real success story that the company loved to tell. Yes, you could actually grow with the company, and you could start behind the counter and end up in the corporate office. Kristine could sell then and she could sell now. She sold me this job right then and there, and, in an instant, my life changed yet again.

I would wake up every morning at about 6:30 a.m. to shower and blow dry my hair to frame my face layered with every product I sold. Then I would stand in front of my closet in a panic about what to wear. Antique house dresses were replaced with corporate suits. No one saw these suits beneath my lab coat, but I had better look the part in case I had a spontaneous meeting with the buyers or company management.

This meant shopping for the first time in my adult life in a real department store with the help of an employee discount and loving co-workers to guide me. I discovered Tahari and the Tahari sales staff. They patiently put together three ensembles that I wore the heck out of throughout this entire chapter. After I dressed the part in front of my mirror, I would walk to the subway with my huge company-branded shoulder bag like a prop carried by a character in a stage play. I would always arrive at the counter bright and early to greet my sales staff, sell alongside them, and perform additional duties that would earn me that magic number on the calculator screen. I never quite earned that magic number, Kristine.

This meant little time for friends and no more boys. My Cabaret acts would take longer to develop, rehearse, promote, and perform, but now the audience would be filled with my fellow retail sisters. This convent of lab coats came in handy on many levels.

I was an executive now. I embraced this role with gusto, like a new part in a musical. I remember loving it when people on the subway looked at me as if I were important. I was fancy now. My shoulder bag was packed with big binders, folders and highlighter pens.

Kristine gave me a great piece of advice. When I asked her how I was going to win over this staff of ladies who were more experienced and in some cases, older than I, she told me this: "Hang back and do everything they have to do, but do it better. Wait a good month and don't manage them at all. Get to work first, clean the counters, stock the shelves, perform consultations on anyone walking by the counter and never say, 'Let me know if you need anything.' Don't let a possible sale or a build of a sale slip through your fingers. Be the last to take lunch and take the shortest lunch, don't take a break if you can, and be the last to leave at the end of the day. After you have earned their respect as a co-worker, begin to manage."

She was brilliant. This advice worked. In about three months time I had built a team at that little counter just off the escalators, but there was a price. I was always tired. Pretending that I cared if we "beat last year's figures" or if "my girls" were ten minutes late returning from lunch, was exhausting.

More importantly, I could not count to save my life. I would enter the stock room to count each and every lipstick, and I swear they would all have had babies since I counted before. I would know that we had sold dozens of Currant Stain Lipstick in the past month. Heck, I sold dozens of Currant Stain Lipstick each month myself, but according to my calculations, we had not sold one single tube. Instead, my calculations showed that the darkness of the locked stockroom made a sexy breeding ground for more little Currant Stain babies to be born.

It was dreadful.

It would take me hours to complete what other hotshot Counter Managers could master in a morning. I was not like the other managers for the other brands. They shared the same red nails and *click, click, click* calculating talents as Kristine. They were not sitting up in the cafeteria sweating before the buying meetings, knowing all would witness the caked-on layers of white-out which were unable to conceal my many failed counting attempts.

I remember my trusted employee, Andie offered to help me. She knew I was in over my head. She would make sure that there was enough coverage at our little counter, knock on the door and then squat down next to me in the dark stock room. Bless her! She made sense out of my mess. While trying hard to stay in character, Andie would look deep into my eyes and ask, "When is your next show, Meg?"

She and her husband met when they were both accountants. She sold cosmetics while she and her hubby tried to make a baby. These connections were worth my moments of humiliation. Andie got pregnant in time, but practiced her mothering on me. She gave me the courage to set up a meeting with Kristine, but only after I had managed to pull off one gift event as a Counter Manager, just one. She encouraged me to give myself that win. I could lead a team to meet the sales goal, improve morale and customer service standards all while my lipsticks in the stock room continued to make more babies.

So, I led one gift event as a manager, complete with my old Associate Consultant freelance buddies working alongside me. My team trusted me and worked hard. I loaded us all up with plenty of sugar and caffeine to sell, sell, sell and reach that goal. They were honest when they were late and I was honest that I was in over my head. There is a lesson there.

Once gift was over, Kristine and I met in that God forsaken cafeteria, but this time I wasn't acting. I told her I was struggling and that I was wasted in the stock room looking for baby lipsticks. I loved the company and would there be some way to create a role for me tapping into what I was good at?

This is where we add gritty Kristine to my list of city angels. She responded that I had grown as a Counter Manager, and although she was very disappointed, she understood. She saw the pale fatigue on my face that matched the white out caked columns of the stock control book each month. My admission could not have been a real surprise.

Kristine decided to move me downstairs to the main counter to serve as Resident Trainer. I would be a counter version of dear Beverly. I would sell alongside the existing staff to raise their customer service standards and inspire new hires to follow suit. Although I was relieved that this particular chapter came to an end, to this day I am proud of my short stint as Counter Manager. It kicked my behind in the best sense of the word. I learned to lead through humility, humor, and trust. I did not hide my failures. Instead of quitting, I asked for help as well as a role that would allow me to continue to contribute.

Before we move on, I must share what Irene taught me. Irene and Kristine were great friends and grew up together behind the counters of greater New York. Irene had been the main floor Counter Manager, but was recently promoted to be an Account Executive. I was brought in to manage the third floor because the existing manager, Tamar, was to take Irene's main floor position.

Irene made the brand look hot. She towered over everyone with her Bumble and Bumble permanent of curls that framed her perfect red smile. She wore high heels to support the best legs I had ever seen. She had her lab coats taken in at the waist and hemmed well above the knees. Betsy Johnson frills would peak out from her polyester white and wink at every store employee, which she knew by name. She was the popular, cool girl in this return to high school experience called cosmetics.

One day, Irene witnessed me announcing how overwhelmed I was in my new position. She cut me off with, "Flather, stop advertising all you don't know. Pretend you know it, keep your mouth shut and go learn it." Wow! What a woman!

Years later I saw Irene at one of Violet's parties. She was happily married to Matt. They met in the stock room and went on to build a family. Instead of Currant Stain Lipsticks, they actually made beautiful babies together.

Here I Go

I'm too good at counting losses
Counting lessons to get through
And looking on the bright side
Of what I'll never get from you

You dare to stand before me
Reaching
As I say goodbye
But where were you
When I was wanting
Begging you to try?

So here I go again
Another road
Another end
Some remedies to mend
And I cannot call you friend

And here I go again
Another road
Another end
Some remedies to mend
And I cannot call you friend

Easily I could just slip in through
Your melancholy blue
Like an old familiar song
I know all the words to

But a brighter melody awaits
For me to sing and play
If I decline this dance with you
This dance with yesterday

So here I go again

Another road
Another end
Some remedies to mend
And I cannot call you friend

And here I go again
Another road
Another end
Some remedies to mend
And I cannot call you friend

And I can't go back
I can't go back
I can't go back
Although I've memorized the way
I gotta remain on track
Remain on track
Take a breath
And stay, stay, stay, stay
Stay

The truth is that I really miss
The one I haven't met
He's waiting 'round the bend
He's gonna help me to forget
'Til then I count my losses
Count my lessons to get through
Looking on the bright side
Of what I'll never get from you

So here I go again
Another road
Another end
Some remedies to mend
And I cannot call you friend

Here I go again

Another road
Another end
Some remedies to mend
And I cannot call you friend

Here I go again
Another road
Another end
Some remedies to mend
And I cannot call you friend

Here I go again
Another road
Another end
Some remedies to mend
And I cannot call you friend

Chapter Ten

Just one of the girls to learn more about boys

I was now 25 years old and still a virgin. Between working alongside ladies in lab coats and singing in West Village Cabarets, straight available men were hard to come by.

It was spring, 1989. My brother was now engaged and there was a party at my parent's home to celebrate the engagement. Rog had met a fellow cast member from my second production of *Nine*. When I went off to England to perform a second production of *Godspell*, they started dating. By my return, they were serious.

There I was sitting alone on my parent's couch amidst a sea of couples. The big, bold diamonds resting upon the left hands of just about every woman in the room made me feel very much alone. I was once again reminded that I was the outsider looking in, who marched to the beat of her own drum. This fact made me feel exotic while singing on the Cabaret stage or from behind the cosmetic counter, but it made me feel pathetic now. Before this October wedding I needed to fix this. I needed to get this thing taken care of. I needed to lose my virginity to someone, anyone, stat.

Jacob was sitting on the chair to my left as I sat alone on the couch. He was a tall, lanky red head who grew up with my brother's fiancé. He was also a producer who lived and worked in Queens. A Woody Allen/Diane Keaton banter quickly and effortlessly began between us. He was witty, smart and intrigued by my alternate life style of selling cosmetics to enable me to sing in West Side clubs. I think he found it refreshing that I was not focused on planning a nuptial event to take place in the same catering hall as all his peers, blocks from where they had all grown up.

Still strutting my Capezio dance boots and antique jewelry, I was now sporting my own Bumble and Bumble bob, dyed red, and a sizable list of cosmetics on my face. At the very least, Jacob found me colorful.

He was the straight man (literally!) on the edge of his seat, entertained by my *Annie Hall*-like monologues. He got me through this sea of engagement rings and asked for my number. I was not expecting his call. I was just happy to have gotten through this party in one piece. Other than a crush in the fourth grade, I did not have much experience with straight men.

This crush moved to our town in the summer of 1973. At the age of nine, he had an old soul sparkle that danced from very knowing eyes. On the first day of the fourth grade, I remember finding countless reasons to pass his desk. I was drawn to him and felt that I had known him for lifetimes even though I never really talked to or understood boys. I could only examine my shoelaces when a smiling boy passed my seat in class or on the bus to and from school each day. Indeed, I was what mom called, "a slow bloomer."

I had heard through the grapevine that when some older boys made fun of my early directorial efforts behind my back, it was my crush that defended my talent and my crush who told them to stop. He also was the first boy to "ask me out" over the phone. My older sisters did not have boyfriends yet. How could I jump past them? I loved my Barbies, my doll house, my show tunes, but boys? What would I say to boys? What would I do with boys? I had heard about fifth grade couples hanging out behind the Star Market after school. I didn't know how to hang out? What was hanging out? I had a backyard musical to direct.

So, I declined.

While sitting on my parents' bed whispering "No, we are too young" into their clunky black, rotary phone, my heart broke for the very first time. I would watch Beth who had braces go out with him instead of me. During the late spring of the sixth grade he announced that his family was moving away that summer. On the last day of school he approached me with his new address perfectly written on a white small card. "Keep in touch," he said.

I kept in touch all right. I used his address as a journal, a depository for every emotion felt for the next decade. These pages would be my safe place to dream big or confide about my butterflies battled daily, walking the junior high school corridors and high school cafeteria floors. I was not like the other girls and he would read all about it.

As I journeyed through junior high school, high school, college and

Summer Stock theatre, little did my crush know that I cast him in the role of an invisible boyfriend to take me off the hook when others were passionate, progressing, partnered.

Over the decades, some letters came my way and there were late night phone calls too. A deep, masculine voice would begin to record a message after the beep at two or three in the morning. I would jump out of bed to pick up the receiver just in time. My only straight male friend would laugh at my jokes and listen patiently to my battles. The elementary school protector who defended me then, defended me now. From time to time, platonic reunions took place when work brought him to New York or when he could hear in my weary voice that I needed a break from my city street-pounding existence.

So, back to the spring of 1989, one of those platonic plans to see my crush came up when Jacob called to take me out for the first time. When I heard the intrigue in his voice, I allowed Jacob to jump to all the wrong conclusions. When I added that I was still a virgin, the fun truly began. He was determined to deflower this virgin before I boarded the plane. Whether he was wild about me or charged up by this imaginary competition, I cannot really say. All I knew is that this hunt was a huge boost to my ego and remedied that dreaded sea of diamond engagement rings I was to navigate on my brother's wedding day, just five months later.

Three days before I was to fly, Jacob and I were on the phone. "Just come over. We won't do anything."

Right. Sure.

So, I took the R train to Astoria and walked many blocks to his apartment, decorated with antique furniture covered in plastic. When he opened the refrigerator to offer me a drink, I saw cans and cans of "No Frills Beer" stacked on the bottom shelf. He was this fancy producer? What was with the plastic and no name beer?

Well, I think I had a couple of those no name beers and found myself too sleepy to journey back to Manhattan. Jacob insisted we would not "do" anything if I slept over. Just a little snuggling and then right to sleep.

Right. Sure.

So, then it happened. I was 25. On the morning of my father's birthday, May 24th, Jacob took care of "it." He knew the enormity of this event and was so flattered to be the one to finally take care of it. Being the hopeless romantic that I am, I felt completely changed. I was a whole new Meg. I was woman. Hear me roar. I roared with glee all the way back to Manhattan, calling my parents from the subway pay phone to tell them the news. In their sweet, awkward, "Do we really need to hear this?" way, they congratulated me.

I got myself back to the apartment, showered and changed in time to make it to my evening shift at the counter. As I made my way to the large, clinical bay, all my sisters in white noticed a glow to my skin and a sparkle in my eye. They saw the caked on concealer around my eyes trying to camouflage the fact that I had zero sleep the night before. I never lacked sleep. I was "in bed by 10 Flather."

"Meg? Meg? What's up?"

"I did it. We did it."

"No way! No way!"

"Hey, everyone, Meg finally did it!"

So, it goes. Around the counter and probably the whole cosmetic floor, the news spread and everyone celebrated that their beloved virgin had grown up. All through my shift, as I leaned down to pull a Currant Stain Lipstick out of a drawer or reached up to remove a yellow lotion off a top, glass shelf, I felt different and loved every minute of it. I was part of the tribe. I was not on the outside looking in, show tune, Peace Corps, Barbie doll-loving Meg. I was inside the group, the center of attention, and so very relieved.

At about 6 p.m., a huge bouquet of long stem red roses made its way through the main floor, bound for our counter. All the glass mirrors behind our white Formica world, usually reflecting lab coats and sterile packaging, got shots of red. Red, red, plush and sexy roses floated into our little world. Everyone cheered as they knew they were from my suitor, the man who did the deed, dear Jacob. Jacob, who I will never thank enough for making the whole experience so validating and worth waiting for, right down to the roses for all the girls to envy.

— I still took that trip just a few days later to see my old friend, the crush. As he was driving, I told him my big, big news. He was so happy for me and relieved for himself, he yelled out the open car window, "Flather did it! Flather did it! Flather did it!" I believe he honked the horn too.

Needless to say, within about a month of the momentous event, Jacob broke up with me. I think he said something like I was "too positive" or "too happy" for him. It was a short, summer courtship about one thing and one thing only. But I will always be thankful to Jacob for taking care of that one thing with respect, care, and roses.

I did go to my brother's wedding dateless. Thankfully, Dad knew to twirl me around the dance floor, reminding me of the other fish in the sea, waiting to meet his Margaret. I remember the huge sense of comfort and safety I felt dancing with Dad that October day. This new woman was still her father's little girl. Dad would always be my safe place to come home to when the fish I counted on changed their minds and swam away.

Angel in My Pocket

Ooh, it waits for you
Ooh, it waits for you

I meet you at the corner
Caffeine and conversation
I feel my heart accelerate
My laughter get a thrill

Your eyes consume with magic tales
That lift
And entertain
Oh, time will you stand still?

'Cause like the cobblestones in Soho I can walk to
Like the clouds in the horizon I can fly through
It doesn't mean that I must have you
Like an angel in my pocket as I roam
That I visit
That I visit
Then go home

Does it feel like second prize
Or crumbs upon the plate?
This chance
And every dance is worth
The worry and the wait

Surrender to the complex
Multi-color shade of gray
The undefined banter
And the play

'Cause like the cobblestones in Soho I can walk to
Like the clouds in the horizon I can fly through
It doesn't mean that I must have you

Like an angel in my pocket as I roam
That I visit
That I visit
Then go home

And I do not need to climb in to
The boat you sail to sea
The boat you built to sail with her
Oh, I will sail with me
I will sail with me

'Cause like the cobblestones in Soho I can walk to
Like the clouds in the horizon I can fly through
And it doesn't mean that I must have you
Like an angel in my pocket as I roam
That I visit
That I visit
Then go home

Tom Sawyer
And a teacher
A monk
A leprechaun
Romantic bandit on your horse
You neverending song

All tucked into the corner
Way up on the avenue
Caffeine and conversation waits for you
Caffeine and conversation waits for you
Caffeine and conversation waits for you
Why does it wait for you?
Ooh, it waits for you
Ooh, it waits for you
It waits for you

Chapter Eleven

"But I don't speak French!"

Tamar was the Counter Manager while I was the resident Beverly. Tamar had served in the Israeli army, was a focused leader and worked as hard as she loved. She also became a dear friend. When a cosmetic brand founded by a French fashion designer came knocking on her door to woo her away from our counter of lab coats, Tamar was ready to be wooed. She also wanted her Cabaret-singing "Megaleg" to come with her. Somehow she convinced the French that I was a makeup artist ready for prime time.

So, I said farewell to the lab coat and now was ready to wear a polyester pink blouse and black wrap skirt every day for the next few years, with pride, purpose, and panache.

Irene's wise words rang in my head. "Flather, stop advertising all you don't know. Pretend you know it, keep your mouth shut, and go learn it." I was never trained as a makeup artist. I did not speak a word of French. I had never stepped foot into this high end, prestigious store, and had no clue why anyone would spend $25 for a lipstick. I remember thinking that my Con Edison electric bill was about $25 dollars each month. Electricity or a lipstick? Are you kidding me? No, they were not. Apparently, it was worth every, single penny, and I had better get used to that fact. Like Tamar, I was ready for a change and was determined to grow myself into this brand, this new store and tap all my acting chops to fool everyone.

Beneath chandeliers and surrounded by columns, mirrors, and plush carpeting, in this new store we serviced the very rich and famous. There was no loud, thumping music or women in black spraying shoppers with the latest fragrance. This was exclusive retail taking place in a Fifth Avenue mansion turned luxury goods department store, just steps away from Central Park. Imagine applying cosmetics in a palace sitting room. That is what my first day in polyester pink was like.

You had to have about seven transactions to make your sales goal each day. A typical sales goal was $2,000. That meant that each shopper had to walk away purchasing roughly $300 of what you sold. That is a lot of lipstick! How was I going to make this goal?

Well, I would remove all traces of her existing makeup and apply toner, serum, day cream, recommend a night cream, and apply an eye cream. Next her primer, foundation, loose powder, as well as a pressed powder for her purse, blush, brow powder, three shadows, cake liner, as well as mascara. Then a lip liner, lipstick, gloss, and matching nail enamel. Then what fragrance was "she"? Well, she had to choose a fragrance and then purchase the matching shower cream, body cream and talc to go with it. At the end of all this she walked away with roughly $300 of merchandise.

The huge lesson that Tamar and I learned was not to stop the sale. "Don't try to save them money, Meg. They are not you. They do not live like you. Let them spend. They will tell you when to stop."

This was huge for me. I would wake up in my little apartment in Greenwhich Village and take the bus to work. I would watch the neighborhood change by the time the bus reached the mansion. At the start of my morning journey, my bus would be packed with numerous skin tones and accents. Artists and exhausted yuppie parents would be rushing their children on and off the bus to school as they made their way to work. Half way up Madison Avenue, the family-owned delicatessens and dry cleaning establishments were replaced by clothing boutiques and fancy hair salons. My bus would empty out and it would be "the ladies who lunched" seated to my right and my left.

I was fascinated by these ladies. I fell in love with their Louis Vuitton bags, Hermès scarves, and Ralph Lauren and Armani suits. I took note of their European shoes that perfectly matched their handbags, belts, and watch bands. Daily I saw what real taste looked like. It meant simple, clean lines accompanied by one great piece of jewelry with the accessories perfectly balanced, creating a collage of class. This shopper taught me all that I value today about fashion. Subtly frame a couple of special ornaments rather than walk about town like a living Christmas tree.

At this pivotal time in my life, I also learned that "money can't buy it." I did meet the fulfilled, happily married and lively customer, but I also served the shopper pulling out her husband's Platinum American Express card as punishment for the affair she thought he was having with a woman half her age. Spending his money on cosmetics she didn't need was revenge. She would never leave him as she refused to live without the comforts the partnership provided, but she would get even. Purchase by purchase, I was the accomplice, the enabler in her shopping crime of passion.

I remember listening to these suspicions knowing that in my locker I had one token for the bus trip home, just enough money for my Diet Coke and diet ice cream lunch and my small brown rice with peanut sauce dinner. In these moments I felt wealthier than all of them. I had a dream. My wealth was measured in the invisible world of music and a project to look forward to. I always had a show scheduled and this got me through the hours of patting age-defying serums into their brow lines and around their sad eyes.

At this stage of the game I was growing my reputation in the Cabaret community. I had expanded my mailing list and received some promising reviews. There was always a stack of show invitations piled under the cash register drawer to hand out to customers at the close of each sale. Few of my customers ever attended my shows, but they were sincere when complimenting my efforts and focus. In these moments, the difference in our worlds was made clear. I didn't lunch with the ladies who lunched. I had a rehearsal with Christian to look forward to and a show to promote.

In my polyester pink I was free. I consider this realization to be the second great gift of my days working for the French. The first gift was the family of friends that I made then and still count on to this day.

The counter of lab coats and yellow moisturizers was huge. You could get lost behind that sea of Formica and avoid any co-workers that challenged your mood, but this new counter was the size of about four bath tubs. I shared those four bath tubs with a cast of co-workers who became my family.

I remember the moment I knew I loved Lynn.

I was leaning over the lipstick drawer looking for #66 lipstick as we were chatting alone for the first time. We were both working the Thursday night shift, the store was virtually empty and management was nowhere to be seen. I was telling her how I lived on the diet ice cream sold just up the street from the employee exit. Lynn howled, "Me too! I don't care if it is made of plastic! It's 100 calories a serving, damn it!"

In that moment Lynn became my new safe place.

Lynn was tough, street smart, smoked cigarettes on her break, and would threaten to beat up any man or woman who ever hurt my feelings. In addition to her red headed grit, this female paradox was quite worldly and lived to travel. I got through my day with a performance to plan. Lynn got through her day with the trip to India to plan. She was the only child of two hard-working parents who poured everything they had into her, and it showed. Yes, she could curse like a sailor, but she was the one who taught me about the finer things in life. She walked me to the scarf department and demanded that I buy my first Hermès scarf and gave me her Louis Vuitton bag that she carried in high school. (In high school!)

She was an avid reader and watched Public Television. When a tourist came in to shop at our counter, Lynn would know all about the country they were from. She would have miraculously seen a documentary about their homeland just weeks before. She had a knack for languages and that girl could sell!

Each Christmas the French would come out with a new, collectible, jewel compact. These "hope diamonds" came in a beautifully silken lined box and were sold for $135 each. Lynn took great pride in selling more of these trinkets that anyone who worked alongside her. When she ran out of real inventory, she would sell the tester. When she had a customer salivating at the thought of purchasing "the last one," she would give me that Lynn look and ask, "Meg, can you check in the back to see if we have one more left?" That meant I was to sneak the un-used tester into my pocket, then go to the back, wipe it down, put in a fresh puff and wrap it up well. How we giggled like naughty school girls as we wished our lucky winner a "happy holidays," watching her sashay through the department, holding on tight to her purchase.

What I cherished most about Lynn was that she taught me I could be cranky, moody, depressed, heart broken or full of vigor, sass, and ambition. I had absolute permission to be Meg and Meg only. The intimacy of this small workspace forced me to be myself. I had no choice. Lynn could read my face, voice, and mind. She had no patience for "nice nice" and told me to "Cut the crap and tell me what is wrong, Meg."

Lynn covered for me when I auditioned for commercials. Through one of my Cabaret acts I actually got an agent. That meant I would get my audition schedule the day before and then Lynn and I would strategize. How would I work my shift and attend all my auditions without anyone upstairs taking any notice? I would wake up in the morning and run to the first audition before my shift, and then dash to the employee locker room and remove my "Young Mom" laundry detergent commercial ensemble to throw on my polyester pink for the first half of the day. Then at lunch, I would dash back to the employee locker room, remove my pink, put on my "Working Mother" credit card commercial ensemble and jump in a taxi bound for the second audition on Broadway and 19th Street. Then I would grab a cab back to the mansion, throw on my pink one final time and head back to the counter often a good ten minutes late. Lynn would cover for me the whole time I was gone.

"Where is Meg?"

"Oh, she is in the stock room counting lipsticks."

"OK. But I want to see her when she gets up here."

Magically as I dashed back to the counter, Lynn would have a customer in the chair, ready for me to sell to. By the time management was approaching the counter to drill me about my absence, I was deep in a make-over. Then somehow the shopper in the chair would buy everything I put on her face. Management would witness these huge sales and walk away, dismissing any question about this Flather girl and her mysterious lunch schedules.

Lynn also nursed my broken heart.

I met Doug on the subway platform the day before Marathon Sunday, the week following my brother's wedding. I was heading to my parents home after a voice lesson to do my laundry. I would always go home with the excuse that I needed to do my laundry, when in truth I was having a hard time. Mom and Dad played along. They would buy that their washer and dryer were so much better than the laundromats in my neighborhood, but what would take place was a proper dinner, a pep talk and taxi fare home. This melancholy, hopeful time in my twenties was so confusing. Moments of feeling that I was an adult about to take over the world of cosmetics and Cabaret were followed by moments of wanting to crawl back into my 1972, pink and white bedroom complete with Shirley Temple smiling at me from the poster on the wall.

There was a street musician performing on the subway platform, and I stopped to listen. So did Doug. The Downtown R train arrived and when we both sat down we began to talk.

"That is what I want to do."

"What is that?"

"I want to sing my own songs one day."

Then the train broke down and we found ourselves walking in the same direction. Doug walked me all the way to my parents' home on East 20th Street. We exchanged numbers and a kiss. The next night I was awoken by my roommate.

"Meg, a Doug is downstairs wanting to come up and see you."

Doug walked through the door with flowers, food, wine and we stayed up all night talking and doing a few other things. My roommate allowed me to break our "No overnight guests" rule. She knew how much I needed this distraction.

Doug was a tall, light-eyed film school student who supported himself modeling and catering. He grew up in Connecticut and reminded me of a young Jimmy Stewart which meant he was my type. He was a great listener and seemed charmed by my over analysis and inability to get to the point of a story. We had a whirlwind courtship for about five days. He arrived at work one night with extra socks, underpants, razors and shaving cream. He wanted to play house as much as I did and asked for a spare key to my apartment. I was in heaven, certain that I had met my soul mate, but on day five I got a call to meet him "to talk."

Doug tried to break up with me on the fifth day of this whirlwind. Instead of trusting that he knew what he wanted and making my way out of the restaurant with only a slightly disappointed heart, I proceeded to manipulate Doug to stay in a relationship with me for the next two years. I think we broke up fourteen times. I just would not listen.

Lynn witnessed all of these endings and beginnings. I would find many creative ways to woo Doug back into my web. I would take acting classes with his teacher, hire him to paint my bathroom and when he showed up to prime the walls, I knew to wear my tightest jeans. Doug didn't stand a chance.

The phone would ring at the counter. Witchy Lynn would hear Doug's "break up" voice and with a warning look in her eyes, would hand me the phone in silence. She always knew when I was going to have one of those nights. Lynn always knew.

I would hear his "We have to talk" and head straight to the drug store on my way home from work to pick up a bottle of NyQuil. Doug was going to break up with me again, which meant quite a bit of crying was to follow. This low budget Judy Garland knew to knock myself out in order to function at work the next day. Selling those $25 lipsticks and $135 compacts took energy. God bless Lynn. She went through this break-up drill all of the fourteen times that Doug "had to talk."

Lynn walked every step with me, never judging, never complaining. She had her version of the same tale with Grant. Lynn and I took turns being the strong one for the other, feeding the other, medicating the other, moving

70

the other, dragging the other out of hiding, and most importantly, unconditionally loving the other like no man ever could.

Doug and I finally broke up just after Christmas. Bill Clinton had just been elected president and a new day in America had begun. Doug had helped me make my new apartment on Avenue C and 10th Street a home. Shelves were put up on the kitchen walls, stocked with pots, pans, spices, and food. Doug challenged my calorie-counting ways and helped me make real progress in caring for myself. He introduced me to mentors who strengthened my acting abilities and planted the seeds of my songwriting future. I consider him another trusted chariot driver who was crucial in taking me from point A to point B, but not to fly the total distance by my side.

Doug was gone, my roommate had moved on to her own apartment, and Jacob and my crush had both gotten married. I was completely alone for the first time in my life. I felt a great deal of shame after the fourteen break-ups I put everyone through. I spent two years running after someone who did not love me and that could not be healthy.

Days after the final break-up, my brother Roger stood in the entrance of my apartment and said, "He did not love you, Meg. He did not love you." I finally heard it. Next time, he, whoever he was to be, was going to love me. Until then I had quite a bit of necessary loneliness to endure, quite a bit indeed.

Flying Boy

Bumped into your friend
He said there's someone new
How I pray for her
How I hope for you
Well, you left me years ago
There were demons to control
You said it wasn't me
I forgave the years you stole

Flying Boy living in the maybe
Flying Boy love somebody
Who's it gonna take to set you free?
Who's it gonna take to set you free?

You know, I watched you while you slept
My most hopeful time
For a moment you were possible, available, mine
But with the rude awakening, affections tucked away
No room left in the secrets you whisper through your
Busy, busy, busy, such a busy day

Flying Boy living in the maybe
Flying Boy love somebody
Who's it gonna take to set you free?
Who's it gonna take to set you free?

How many more years
Of Sunday morning break up tears?
How many more years
Locked up behind your fears?
When you can love somebody
Love somebody
When you can love somebody
Love somebody

Bumped into your friend
He said there's someone new
How I pray for her
How I hope for you

You know what to do
You know what to do
You know what to do
You know what to do

Love somebody, love somebody
Will you love somebody, love somebody
Will you love somebody, love somebody

Chapter Twelve

"Why are you here?"

In our family, asking for help was something we did not do. We were told repeatedly that we had Mayflower lineage and that my mother was related to William Witherspoon who signed the Declaration of Independence. The Flather family's management of the Boott Mills in Lowell, Massachusetts played a pivotal role in the Industrial Revolution. Framed stoic faces hung from the walls of my grandparents' homes. If I stared at these expressions long enough, they would almost come to life to scold me and say, "Keep a stiff upper lip, Margaret, and pull up your boot straps. You are a Davis. You are a Flather. Stop this complaining and count your many blessings."

However, this Puritan way of managing pain wasn't working now. I was grieving a loveless relationship fueled by drama. I was mortified and ashamed of this fact. There was something missing in me that younger, healthy women seemed to possess. I chose men *because* they were unavailable, *because* they did not want me. I was broken. Like a defective blow dryer or vacuum cleaner, I had a missing part. I needed to go get that part. I needed help again.

I had some therapy when I was about twenty years old. My brother, Roger, had just returned from two years serving in the Peace Corps in Zaire, Africa. It was clear at first glance that something was wrong with his Meg. Fueled by only five hundred calories a day, I was addicted to taking too many dance classes a day, while juggling my college classes and waitressing shifts. I weighed about 115 pounds. Roger had good reason to be alarmed.

"What the hell is going on with Meg? Can't anyone see how thin she is?"

An appointment was scheduled, and I did some good preliminary work with my first therapist. We explored my relationship with food and control. I would proudly never get that thin again.

My mother tells the story of living on ice cream as a teenager and weighing ninety pounds on her wedding day. Vanity, perfectionism, and control were passed on passions for the women in our family, and secretly for the men as well. My father would binge. Late at night when we were tucked into our beds, he would consume anything edible in the icebox. Standing in a dark kitchen with only the light of the refrigerator as company, my father consumed frozen hot dogs and mayonnaise sandwiches. My mother tried to control his weight and his blood pressure. "Meg, go see if your father is breathing. Are you dead, Rog?" I would go check his breathing for her and report back that he was very much alive. She was so afraid of losing him to a heart attack. We never imagined that cancer would ultimately take him from us.

Back in the 1970s, Mom put a locked cabinet up in the laundry room to store the Twinkies, Pringles, and Pop Tarts that she wanted us to enjoy. Our portions were carefully rationed each day before she went to work. Finally, Roger and I began to climb on top of the dryer with a screwdriver and unhinge the cabinet door ourselves. We sneaked out just enough salt and sugar which would go unnoticed for months. It was partly exhilarating and partly pathetic. Thinking back, I am amazed at how criminal we felt while feeding ourselves. Ultimately the hinge broke. That was the end of the cabinet and the Twinkies. When I had friends over to play, I was ashamed of our empty refrigerator. I would put covered pots, pans and various household-cleaning products upon the shelves to keep our family secret. I would open the refrigerator door quickly and say, "We only have leftovers. Let's go to your house."

Joni and I had little in common. She was bookish, and I sang show tunes, yet I would go play with her while her mother produced bakery-bought black and white cookies and cans of cold Pepsi. We would feast in her room to Dionne Warwick's "Do You Know the Way to San Jose?" sounding from her little record player. Just as the song ended, I would announce that I had chores to do and scurry home. When I went on to babysit Joni's younger sister, it seemed that her mother stocked her kitchen shelves just for me. This suburban angel wore bright blue contact lenses that sparkled with quiet generosity.

What started out as a harmless effort to lose ten pounds before the first day of high school, turned into a decade of dieting. I was hooked. Friends would envy my control and unwavering will power. I would eat carrot sticks at parties while they consumed too many bags of Doritos. Later in my twenties, dancers in front of the class mirror would whisper about my Bob Fosse like frame. I was in heaven. This "nice girl" who was raised to believe that competitive girls were too aggressive would quietly win a war of sorts, the war on weight.

Until Roger saw that I was not winning anything.

With the help of this first therapist, I gained ten pounds and kept it on. I was certain that I was all better now when I ended our work a few months after it began.

I never imagined that my dance with deprivation would rematerialize in my choice of men. Like a sponge in a bathtub, I couldn't push it down anymore. After Doug left, my addiction to control popped up with a new face, and this time it was not going away.

I was finally ready for the real therapy work. I was ready for Lana.

Lana's office could not have been further away from my East Village home. This somehow made sense. This time therapy could not be casual, penciled in and then dropped once a new boy showed up. It was not to be quick or easy. It was work this time. I was not placating family or distracting myself from the latest case of break-up butterflies. Everywhere I looked, there I was.

As I waited for the bus, I ignored imagined stiff upper lip lectures from those framed Flather faces lined up in a hallway in my mind. I was to endure whatever test it took to repair or replace that broken piece inside of me. The long commute was my first test, my proof to the universe that I was ready.

So I took the cross town bus from Avenue C and 10th Street to Broadway and 8th Street, and then took the uptown R train to Times Square. Then I transferred to the uptown 1 train and took it to 96th Street. I walked to Riverside Drive and took an elevator to sit with the hum of a sound machine blocking whatever was going on behind the French doors of Lana's office. Each step of the commute felt like payment, payment towards a true self and a life that reflected it.

The French doors opened. The patient before me was crying as she retrieved her coat and opened the door of Lana's suite. With her head down, she said, "See you next week." I remember feeling envious. I wanted to cry too.

Lana was a vision. She was lean and petite and wore wire rimmed glasses and delicate, beaded jewelry. I loved that she had short brown hair like mine, but that hers was cut in a shag-like style, reminiscent of the sitcom mothers in my favorite 1970s television shows. She wore a neutral-colored skirt and blouse with sensible flat shoes. Lana was perfect.

Our session began. First I rambled on about the latest break-up, spinning, running, fighting any real feeling that I was having inside. Then the moment that never happened with any of the other therapists happened. Lana gently cut me off with, "Meg, why are you here?"

Then after a bit of silence I responded, "I guess, well, how do I describe it? I, I can't wear this, this mask anymore. That is what it feels like. Like I am wearing a mask all the time and it is just too heavy. But I am afraid. I am afraid of who is behind it. Actually, I am afraid nothing's behind it."

"Well, let's find out together, Meg. What do you say?"

With that I jumped up and threw my arms around her. Although this went against therapist and new patient etiquette, Lana allowed this moment. I held on to her saying, "Thank you, thank you, thank you." I finally felt safe, heard and protected. I like to think that in that mutual embrace, we both got a sneak peak in to the next sixteen years that we would be so proud of together. How we would laugh, cry, grieve and celebrate Meg together. The student was ready and the teacher knew it. So, we began. I took that bus to the train, to the train, to the avenue, to the elevator, to the waiting room, to the sound machine twice a week, and never looked back.

I am very proud of this work, this commitment, and this admission that I needed help. I didn't have to be afraid of the sad self who hid behind the bright smile. In the safety of Lana's chamber, I practiced pulling that heavy mask down and meeting the little girl living behind it.

I learned to love that little girl. She was crafty, with plenty of pluck. She had misunderstood why parents were so busy and why boys went away. She had exhausted herself with schemes of perfection to remedy these disappointments. After the long road with Lana, that little girl naps quietly within, and a new trusting force navigates the ship.

I don't race from behind, begging to be seen, wanted, and loved. I don't complete impossible schedules and impressive lists to avoid the anxiety within. I wish to create and express my talents because it feels good, because I have something to say. Not for approval. When I walk into a room that feels strange, I won't assume that I am to blame and that I had better start fixing it.

Lana helped me to see that it was not about controlling food, audiences, or boys. I was not going to fix or replace my missing part through dances of control. It was only through my willingness to honestly feel the unintentional abandonment experienced in my youth that I could then pass through to the other side. Lana promised me that if I had the courage to bear every dark feeling with her, I would eventually grow closer to my parents and tap a new and healthy love for myself as well. It works. You can "go home again" if you first face your past while seated in the safety net of a therapist's office.

But here is the real kicker. You must also own how your "stuff" manifests into patterns of behavior that push away personal and professional success in your present adult life. Therapy is not just about mourning childhood loss, but also about taking responsibility for how that loss creates unhealthy dynamics that hurt you and those you try to love today. Your job is to retrain yourself to behave and respond differently when your buttons from the past are pushed. Then before you know it, you demand only the friends, the job and partner that reflect this new self care, this painstaking work. You become authentic for the first time. You "come out of the closet" so to speak.

In my high school yearbook, I chose this Shakespearean quote to sit beneath my photograph, "To thine own self be true." It took me a long time to figure out what that meant, but I got there.

Thank you, Lana, we got there.

Go Home

You hold your breath
In a vanilla room
Vanilla days
Vanilla tomb
Posing in a menagerie
Was this who you
Planned to be?

Close the door
And lock it
Roll the map up
In your pocket
It holds the path
You vowed to take
Against all odds
To stay awake

Little glass ball
China doll
Shatter
Fall to pieces
Scatter
Go home

Little glass ball
China doll
Shatter
Fall to pieces
Scatter
Go home

Where you danced with grass
Beneath your feet
To sounds and smells
Of summer heat

Toasting skies
The sunrise
With wide eyes

The smoke and mirrors
Fade into
The gilded cage
You now peak through
Turn within to tap the grace
Your steps await
To be retraced

Little glass ball
China doll
Shatter
Fall to pieces
Scatter
Go home

Little glass ball
China doll
Shatter
Fall to pieces
Scatter
Go home

Dive into the river
You can find her
Dive into the river
You can find her
Dive into the river
You can find her
Dive into the river
Remember

Little glass ball
China doll

Shatter
Fall to pieces
Scatter
Go home

Little glass ball
China doll
Shatter
Fall to pieces
Scatter
Go home

Little glass ball
China doll
Shatter
Fall to pieces
Scatter
Go home

You hold your breath
In a vanilla room
Vanilla days
Vanilla tomb
Dive into the river
Remember

Chapter Thirteen

Just a little celebrity worship

What was incredible about working at the mansion during the early 1990s, was that it was one of the "it" places for celebrities to shop. We were trained to stand tall, look straight ahead and remain silent. We were to by no means behave like a fan when assisting a celebrity with their purchases, but not me. I found my own, quiet or not so quiet way to communicate what their talent meant to me.

I helped Cyndi Lauper purchase the fairest shade of foundation and Suzanne Vega, the fairest loose powder. I gave Mary Tyler Moore and Shirley MacLaine directions to the Ladies Room. I watched a very young Mariah Carey sample another brand's eye cream and let Johnny Depp and Winona Ryder privately peruse our nail polish testers. Little did I know then that I needed to watch her closely, as some of those testers may have gone missing! Jane Pauley always bought #52 lipstick from me, the perfect blend of coral and pink, and I passed Oprah examining very expensive accessories.

Journalist, Sylvia Chase of *60 Minutes*, seasonally bought all her on-camera cosmetics from me. She would sit in my chair for the longest time, trusted all my suggestions and bought far too much product in order to help me reach my sales goal. Years later, she attempted to attend my Cabaret debut at The Ballroom. She missed the show, but sat at the bar with my band affirming their courage to make music at all costs. She is what my mother would call, "a class act."

I watched Susan Lucci test moisturizer on her daughter's chin, and as Jessica Lange was strolling to the elevator, I broke the store rule and told her how much her talent inspired me. She was very gracious, but kept moving. I believe she was starring with Alec Baldwin in the Broadway production of *A Streetcar Named Desire.*

Then there was that one, magical Christmas Eve.

I was standing in front of our tester unit hoping to draw some shoppers. This is what they wanted us to do. If the store was quiet, we would have to stand in front of our counters, with a "May I show you some new winter colors this evening?" Oh, how I hated doing this. I always felt so desperate. Anyway, it was about one hour to closing. After a long, grueling holiday schedule of additional shifts and gift wrapping around the clock, we had "decked" more than enough halls, to say the least.

There I was leaning against my shadows counting the minutes until I could head over to my parents' Christmas Eve celebration, when I saw a tall dark man who needed assistance. The round glass table that displayed expensive pine-smelling candles had been left unattended. I was not supposed to leave my counter, but this gentleman clearly needed assistance, and nothing was going on at my counter.

"May I help you with the candles, sir?"

With that, the gentleman turned around. It was John F. Kennedy Jr.

My heart still pounds as I tell this story today. My father was Ted Kennedy's roommate at Harvard back in the early 1950s. My father went on to become a Peace Corps Staff Director in Malaysia because of his admiration for Ted Kennedy's older brother, President John F. Kennedy. My parents already had two beautiful daughters and one son. They didn't need more children. I believe I was born because of the Peace Corps, because of President Kennedy, just like John-John! We were connected and were supposed to meet! These were the thoughts spinning around in my brain as I looked up at this strappingly handsome, charismatic man, born only a few days apart from my brother. Oh, this meeting was supposed to happen. It was destined to take place. Merry Christmas, to me!

Thank God he interrupted my inner talk with, "Yes, I could really use your help. I was thinking that my mother would love one of these candles."

His mother, Jackie?

Now the fantasy was spinning out of control. I considered myself to be the poor man's Jackie Onassis, the Jackie O of retail and Cabaret. This was truly destiny at work.

"Yes, these are beautiful and they last a really long time. Here is one already gift wrapped and in a shopping bag for you, ready to go."

Then he handed me his credit card so that I could go into the back and have Jackie's candle rung up. I ran into the back and yelled out, "John-John! This is for John-John, I mean Jackie!"

Everyone laughed and poked fun at me, and I delighted in every minute of the madness. This backstage register and gift wrapping station behind the chandeliers and plush carpeting was where we would all go to avoid management, snack on chips, down a needed cup of coffee, take off our shoes, and most importantly, gossip.

When I returned to the glass table to get John-John's signature, I saw that he was leaving through the revolving doors and out into the slushy snow. I broke the security rule and did not use the employee exit. Instead, I followed him, yelling out into the street, "John-John! John-John!" Surrounded by fur coats, velvet scarves and bustling New Yorkers, I stood in my polyester pink, feeling my black suede flats soak into the December slush. He didn't hear me. He was gone. His tall, dark frame faded into the distance of Fifth Avenue forever.

So, I took his credit card and receipt up to Customer Service.

"This belongs to John F. Kennedy, Jr. He left the store before he could sign the receipt and take back his card. I would be happy to hand deliver it to his home tonight, or Jackie's home. They are certain to celebrate Christmas Eve together, don't you think?"

This was fantasy number two. I would knock on Jackie's Fifth Avenue front door and a butler would open the door to find me in my polyester pink standing in the cold. He would welcome me in and lead me into the grand room, where they would proudly display their ten-foot tall and perfectly decorated Christmas tree. The crackling fire, the haze of holiday lights and the smell of that candle that I had sold her son hours before would warm up my wet suede feet. The butler would proudly announce, "A Miss Margaret Flather is here to see your son, Madam. Apparently, John left his credit card while shopping for your gift."

Then Jackie would somehow recognize my last name. She would have heard about my father's service in the Philippines through Sergeant Shriver, my father's supervisor. She would invite me to stay and would insist that I wear one of her black cocktail dresses and famous pearl necklaces. I would feast at the dining room table next to Caroline and ultimately marry John-John by late summer.

"That will be all, Miss Flather. I will take it from here."

With that, the credit card was whisked out of my hand by the head of Customer Service, and I was back at my counter. Like Cinderella after the ball, my fantasy was over.

But I have the perfect memory of this perfect gentleman. I remember the summer night his plane went missing in the Cape Cod waters of Massachusetts. I took it personally. He was my friend and now he was gone. My dream date for Christmas Eve was gone forever.

You Shine Through Your Father's Eyes

In your eyes there burns a flame
A spirit he will never tame
With hair like strands of summer's gold
A smile so young
A mind so old
How is it that you always know
What took us years to learn and grow?

Each night he may not tuck you in
But oh to see your father grin
When I ask about your day
And how you laughed and how you played
How your wonder and desire
Inspire
His sleeping fire

And for a moment I see how hard he tries
To fight the walls, fight the lies
Oh, what a wonderful surprise
To see you shine through your father's eyes
To see you shine through your father's eyes

Because of you I see him more
You're the key that opens the door
The window to what used to hide
This man so tender, free of pride
Because of you he steps outside
Because of you he steps outside

And for a moment I see how hard he tries
To fight the walls, fight the lies
Oh, what a wonderful surprise
To see you shine through your father's eyes
To see you shine through your father's eyes

You shine
Shine
Shine
Shine

I see how hard he tries
To fight the walls, fight the lies
Oh, what a wonderful surprise
To see you shine through your father's eyes

For a moment I see how hard he tries
To fight the walls, fight the lies
Oh, what a wonderful surprise
To see you shine through your father's eyes
To see you shine through your father's eyes

You shine
Shine
Shine
Shine

Chapter Fourteen

And then there was...

Our circular bay of cosmetic confections was small, but you could still find ways to demand some privacy when feeling a little melancholy. When the store was slow, I always felt melancholy. This idle time would stare me in the face. I was not singing, I was not acting, and I was not creating. I was just waiting. Waiting for someone in need of a new look, and let's face it, waiting for so much more that was not coming any day soon.

When filled with self-pity, I would find my way to the portion of our bay that we rarely used, the half circle that faced the revolving door to the street. On this particular day, as I stood there, in came Barbra Streisand. Yes, the Barbra Streisand. I had always admired and respected her breakthrough career. She started on The Duplex stage like me! But she was not "one of my women." I didn't own any of her albums and went to see her films mainly because friends dragged me along. However, in this moment, as she faced me from across the counter glass, I absolutely fell in love.

I had never seen skin like hers in my life. It was early summer, and Barbra was wearing a long, black, knit sleeveless dress that exposed her neck, chest, and arms. When I took in her face, neck, arms, and perfectly manicured nails, I was struck by her skin. Not a pore, line or mark was to be found. Instead, one endless, golden sea of perfectly moisturized and maintained skin seemed to float before me.

I then took in her perfectly lined eyes, shaped brows and glossy pink lip tone that matched her nails made famous in the movie, *The Way We Were*. Yes, those same nails that brushed the blond locks out of Robert Redford's eyes were resting on my counter, my bay, my melancholy chamber.

"I am here for my personal shopping appointment. Would you let them know that I am here?"

"Absolutely, please come with me."

We walked quietly through the department to the elevators, where the Customer Service telephone was mounted upon the wall. I could feel that all eyes were on me and my new best friend. I slowed down my usual retail pace to stretch and savor the moment.

I picked up the phone and said in a voice loud enough for her to hear, "Ms. Barbra Streisand is here."

I knew that she was a feminist and that Ms. would be the most appropriate title, never Miss or Mrs. for a Democrat who adored our currant president, Bill Clinton. Heavens no!

"Yes, Ms. Barbra Streisand."

(Now here it comes. I took a huge leap of faith with this one.) "You know Barbra Streisand, who deserved an Oscar Nomination for Best Director for *The Prince of Tides*!"

With that, Barbra's head snapped around to finally take a good look at me with an expression that first seemed to say, "Who the hell are you?", but that within seconds melted into a sincere and somewhat vulnerable, "Thank you. Thank you very much."

"Well, it's true!" I said with defiance, like we had known each other for years.

With that, the elevator doors opened. She pushed the button to her floor, gave me a quiet smile, and then looked down as the doors began to close.

All eyes were still on me, thank goodness for that. Our meeting was too short. I wasn't ready to go back to my revolving door sentence and inner lists of all I could be doing if I didn't have to work. I quietly sauntered back to my bay and now stood by the busy station that faced the selling floor. It was time to greet my selling peers and their inquiries regarding my magical encounter with this super star, my new best friend.

After the initial buzz, I leaned against my tester unit with my eyes fixed on that elevator door. She was sure to come down as soon as she was done selecting her new wardrobe. She was sure to come back to my counter and take me to lunch. She was sure to want to sit for hours in a pretentious café, comparing notes on music, comedy, theater, film and even The Duplex stage we both performed upon.

She was sure to ask me to sing back-up vocals for her in her next recording project, or open for her if she was to perform again, or maybe even work me into her next film somehow? At least she would certainly come back to purchase some new pink lip gloss and matching nail enamel? She was sure to, right?

Nope.

That was it.

Barbra was gone.

I like to think that she remembers me. Maybe I was the one who helped her to process and release those Oscar demons once and for all? I know that she left me with a wonderful story and a vision of the most beautiful skin that I have ever seen. This is what I think of when her name comes up: not her voice, not her iconoclastic career, but her skin. Once a shop girl, always a shop girl, I suppose. I mean, come on, great skin trumps all.

Chapter Fifteen

A crosstown bus

The pain of the loss of my boyfriend Doug was lessening, and I was beginning to get into a rhythm of Meg time and Meg missions. I was getting far too much sleep and excelling in my job as a result. My average unit sale was increasing, and my Cabaret career was benefitting from no male distractions.

Christian and I were working beautifully on my solo career with shows entitled, *Life Stories and Portraits*. I was learning that my Cabaret shows were strongest when I told a story or created a character through music. We put together some very clever shows with material that spanned the history of pop, rock, and folk music, and obscure, never-performed show tunes. My retail buddies came to each show and filled the back room of a new venue, Don't Tell Mama. None of my friends were parents yet, the economy was coming back, and the drinks were cheap! If my show was not your cup of tea, it only lasted sixty minutes, which is an advantage of the art form called Cabaret.

When I look back at each chapter following a break-up, the world around me consistently handed me signs that I was right where I was supposed to be. So, why did I always rush back into another relationship as fast as possible? Was it a fear of flight, fear of success?

In my freshman year drama class, our sense memory teacher had us perform a moment alone exercise. He had us shut our eyes and imagine where we would be in ten years. He instructed us to see, smell, and feel that environment. We were instructed to experience every detail and play with it a bit. My imagined future scared me a lot. I was in a dressing room of a theater an hour or so before giving a performance and although I was successful in this vision, I was also very much alone except for Mom in a chair, watching me as I prepared.

This exercise haunted me for the next ten years. Did I have to choose between performing and a man? If I chose performing, I would only have Mom there to support me. Maybe, just maybe, this was why when I felt a surge of creative power and external affirmation; I put a man back in the center of my life. I don't blame any of these gentleman callers for taking part in this dance. This was my dance and my dance alone. It just felt too scary, too hot even, to actually use all my pieces and channel all my focus towards Meg and Meg only.

However, by 1993 I began to try. I savored the creative affirmations by day and endured the empty bed at night.

I had hired a woman who helped Cabaret performers get reviewed. This was a big step for me. I was only paid $18 an hour for retail work, but I wrote her a check. What came out of this transaction was not a review, but a meeting with a commercial agent. The young receptionist for a talent agency came to see my one-woman show and reported back to her colleagues that I was worth a meeting. With the success of the television show, *Seinfeld*, and the rising popularity of Julia Louis Dreyfuss, advertisers were looking for urban, edgy brunettes to play the wives and mothers who squeezed toilet paper, wiped counters, and administered cough suppressant. I was back to auditioning and got a callback after the first one. A new phase of my career had begun. I was now a commercial actress.

I still worked my selling shifts, but now went to several commercial auditions a day. This was tricky, but as I shared earlier, dear Lynn and the store managers looked the other way when I jumped in and out of taxis and my polyester pink. As long as I met my sales goal, all parties let me pursue this new path.

It was a great time. I rehearsed for Don't Tell Mama by night and juggled auditions and average unit sales totals by day. There were three cats now curled up in bed with me as I chatted on the phone with Lynn each night. I wasn't lonely. For a season, I endured the focus on me, just me.

But sometimes, just sometimes, I was reminded of how a man in my life would come in handy.

One night, dear Harriet, (my adventurous, black and white, Natalie Wood meets Karen Black, slightly cross eyed kitty) succeeded at knocking the living room window screen off its track. She then climbed through the small space she created, down the fire escape steps, to the court yard below, behind my Avenue C home.

Now, when Harriet was fixed, the veterinarian unintentionally scratched her vocal chords. She was a rescue kitten who could have been pregnant when I brought her to be fixed. So, the vet had to use a more powerful anesthesia that had to be delivered down her throat in a tube in case he discovered a pregnancy and needed more time for the procedure. So, after this procedure, (and she was not pregnant!) her meow sounded exactly like Demi Moore and only Demi Moore.

So, she succeeded to climb down to the courtyard and when I realized she was not curled up at my feet, I went to the window to hear her Demi Moore meow sound and sound and sound. It was not pretty. Now, I was a hip, fearless East Villager now, who lived in an edgy neighborhood. I even bought kitty litter, cat food and toilet paper at a drug front posing as a deli. The guy behind the counter would ask me what I usually paid for these "props" and would charge me what I told him to charge me. But I was not adventurous enough to go out in to the night to rescue my kitty alone. This is where Roger, my brother and soul mate, earned major points, major points. I called him at about three in the morning and he actually picked up the phone. I explained the emergency and without hesitation, Roger put a coat on over his pajamas, jumped in a taxi and had the taxi wait outside my building. I met him in the lobby in my pajamas, and together we went out into the courtyard to call out to Harriet.

"Harriet. Harriet! Harriet!"

Now imagine the Demi Moore meow.

"Harriet!"

With that she came out from the shrubs, jumped in to my arms and the two of us escorted Roger to his waiting taxi. The next morning Roger called me. He asked, "Did I dream this or did we actually rescue Harriet last night?"

Well, he did not dream it and we did rescue Harriet that night. But that is par for the course for Roger, my life line. Needless to say it was time to start dating.

I met Alan on the crosstown bus.

Alan lived on Avenue B. It was a snowy day in late February, 1993, when I got on the M13 northbound bus that traveled across 10th Street. Alan and I were both minding our own business, he with his guitar and me with my several changes of audition ensembles. A Seeing Eye dog and his master boarded the bus and we were intrigued by this poignant duo and began to talk.

When the bus reached 4th Avenue, we both had to get off to connect with the Madison Avenue uptown bus. Alan helped me off the bus and through a snow drift, like the true gentlemen featured in the black and white films I now watch with Mom on Turner Classic Movies. We began to talk about music. I gave him my card and said, "Please invite me to your next gig."

After a couple of months he called. He left a message asking would I be his guest at his next gig, but would I also like to have dinner in our neighborhood tonight? I hesitated. I loved my new-found independence, but this guy sounded sweet, so sweet. So, I answered, "Yes. Yes, I would love to."

And so it began, the longest relationship I had had up to this point. Alan was a very talented, hard-working musician who was beloved by all those he worked with. He was honorable, intelligent, kind, and true. I would go on to marry Alan. No one had treated me with this level of care. No man had ever loved me this much.

Wake-up Call

It seems as though
A month ago
I didn't stop to question

I had a plan
Some gifts
A smile
A map with some direction

A list of chores
To check each night
With pen
So proud
So finished

Those checks seem less
Important now
The urgency
Diminished

Is it in a book?
The holy book?
My mother's pride?
My lover's look?

Is it in a glowing Times review?
In a church?
Beneath the pew?

Where is it?
Where is it?
Where is it?
Where is it?

I have a home

A job
A name
My health
My tribe
My quest for fame

It seemed to fill
The void before
So what's this voice
Demanding more?

I fight your words
My emptiness
Don't shake my world
It works like this

What is to gain
To go inside?
To search for "I"
To trust your ride?

Well, I'll lose more weight
I'll drink more wine
I'll sleep too late
I'll waste more time

I'll drown you out
Without a trace
I'll call my ex
I'll paint my face

Is it in a book?
The holy book?
My mother's pride?
My lover's look?
Is it in a glowing Times review?
In a church?

Beneath the pew?

Where is it?
I look and look
Where is it?
And look and look
Where is it?
I look and look
Where is it?
And look and look

Is it in a book?
The holy book?
My mother's pride?
My lover's look?
Is it in a glowing Times review?
In a church?
Beneath the pew?

Is it in a book?
The holy book?
My mother's pride?
My lover's look?
Is it in a glowing Times review?
In a church?
Beneath the pew?

Where is it?
I look and look
Where is it?
And look and look
Where is it?
I look and look
Where is it?

Chapter Sixteen

"But I don't know how to write music!"

I was performing my Cabaret acts, singing songs by artists like Joni Mitchell and Mary Chapin Carpenter, when it started to become clear to me that that I was hitting a wall. Why listen to Meg Flather sing "The Circle Game" when you could listen to the master, the goddess herself, sing it?

One night after one of my Don't Tell Mama shows, an acquaintance made fearless by her two-drink minimum approached me. My audience had found their way out of the bar and into taxis, when she approached me as I sipped my complementary glass of Chardonnay. She looked me in the eye and said, "If you don't start writing your own songs, you are going to be a very bitter woman."

Wow.

While that took a great deal of courage to say, I will take full credit for the courage it took me to take it in. Just as I was tempted to shut down this dialogue with, *What I am doing with covers is original*, I knew to shut up, hear it and feel it. Darn it! She was right, but what was I to do? How do you write a song? I don't write songs.

Within a season of this daunting bar encounter, I found myself attending an esoteric study class that met two nights a week in a loft in Soho. Each month the students set goals to do something that they were scared of doing, something that would strongly complement how they lived their daily lives, to wake up from their sleep, or in my case, to rip off that darn mask that I complained to Lana about.

I stood up before this class to set my goal. I was the newest student, and I had never set one of these goals before. My heart was racing, and I couldn't feel my feet as they stood upon the wooden risers that supported rows of folding chairs. These risers held about seventy-five students, and created a semi-circle around the teacher who was seated in a grand chair on the floor.

"I will write lyrics as my goal."

Silence.

The teacher didn't say anything for a long time. He seemed to be watching a montage play behind my eyes detailing every creative regret, roadblock, and lie I had told myself since I wrote that one song performed in every backyard musical I produced as a child in elementary school.

"No. You will also write the music."

"But I don't know how."

"You will figure out how. Twice a week for five weeks you will sit down and write words and music for forty minutes. You will perform a complete song for us in five weeks. Thank you. You can sit down now."

And that was that.

Oh, no! What have I signed up for here? What is this crazy place, and who is this crazy teacher? Yet in that brief, intense exchange, I knew he was right. I bought a small cassette tape recorder the next day. I didn't tell a soul about this experiment and kept every forty minute date with myself for the next five weeks.

I remember the night that I heard my first song play in my head. Honestly, some invisible soul sang every lyric into my ear. I simply repeated what I heard into my little recorder. My first song, "Wake-up Call," must have been written by a ghost. It came too easily and felt like someone else's song. Well, maybe not.

The tone, the vibration, and the energy of this song did not sound like Meg at all. I was happy, I thought. I was positive, I thought. I was upbeat, I thought. How could a minor, haunting song that confronted pretty much every choice I had ever made be the result of this first exercise? The chorus simply asked, "Where is it? Where is it? Where is it? Where is it?" I could not have written this. Well, I did.

Nothing ever was the same after that night. I owe much of my mental health and purpose to the acquaintance at the bar, and to the fierce teacher who was determined to challenge all the things that spin when "happy" Meg is in the room.

That first song also brought me closer to Alan.

We had been dating for just a few months when I first "heard" my first song play in my head. I remember sitting at his dining room table with my humble cassette player, feeling nervous and exposed. What if he hated it? Or worse, what if he just humored me? Well, this moment reflects the enormous character Alan possesses. First he actually liked the song and then we stayed up most of the night finding the chords on his acoustic guitar and recording it on a little home recording studio he kept in the hall closet. From that night on, music became the glue that held our union together.

The next day I took the demo tape to work and played it for my loyal counter of shop girls in the stock room. They were all so supportive and demanded that I keep going. So I did. I continued to write, and Alan continued to find the chords and record humble demo tapes on his dining room table.

On our first date, Alan took me to the dog run in Tompkin's Square Park to watch the dogs play. If you recall, we met on that bus both adoring the Seeing Eye dog tending to his master's every need. So, when it was time to name the band, MY DOG made sense. So, MY DOG was the name of the band, with a halo over the O in DOG. Dog spelled backwards is God, and let's face it, there was a lot of God energy in this huge leap of faith. I was living like Joni Mitchell. I, too, now called myself a singer/songwriter. I was free.

After one tryout of my new material at Don't Tell Mama it was clear that I had to be brave and begin to "gig" rather than create "acts." It was also clear that I had to leave the safety of the Cabaret stage and perform in the clubs downtown like every other band. I played at clubs along Bleeker Street, but finally found a home on the corner of Avenue A and 6th Street. The Side-Walk Cafe had a cool back room that promoted new bands and artists. I submitted a cassette of "Wake-up Call" in hopes of playing in the back room. Within a couple of days the booking manager left a message on my answering machine. He liked "Wake-up Call," and I found a home at The SideWalk for the next ten years. Two of Alan's good buddies supplied our rhythm section (bass and drums), and miraculously I started booking voice-over commercials.

I was not to be one of those commercial actors who made a great deal of money simply to live. It was as if the universe first needed to see that the increase in funds would go towards a creative project. Once the band was formed and an album's worth of songs had been composed, an orange drink campaign hired me to be their voice for roughly five national commercials. That meant I had enough money to go into the studio and record my first album. Supply, demand, request, response. I have been making music with the starry, starry world ever since.

I have a memory of complaining to Rog that I wanted Mom and Dad to fund my first CD. He turned to me and whispered,

"The success is sweeter when it is yours, Meg."

Doggone it, he was right.

Dad used to say, "She who chops her own wood is twice warmed, Margaret. Warmed once because she now has enough wood for the winter, but warmed twice because she has built up a good sweat chopping wood." You have to imagine this being said with the thickest Bostonian accent possible to really experience the total effect.

I get it, I get it. Do it yourself. Don't be like the other girls. My two Rogers in my life made this point very clear and I ended up quoting both of them in my song, "A Song of Roses."

So, I grew my own roses. I grew six roses, well, six albums. I "grew" these albums when I made $20,000 a year and $20,000 a commercial. When I took a creative leap, magic appeared. By magic I mean the help I needed to make my projects come to fruition. I didn't need to be famous; I needed to be creative. And for me that was the point, the only point.

A Song of Roses

When I wanted rescuing
My brother made it clear
"It is sweeter when it's yours"
He'd whisper in my ear

And "She who chops her own wood"
My father would recite
"Is warmed up by the sweat of it
And what burns through the night"

Take the thorns
The heat and toil
The time to plant
And till your soil
This, my family recipe
For growing your own roses
Naturally

Younger faces come my way
Asking for advice
I'm the one who took some knocks
The one who tried things twice

"Don't follow all the others"
I bellow to the rafters
"The ones who wait for roses
And happy ever afters"

Take the thorns
The heat and toil
The time to plant
And till your soil
This, my family recipe
For growing your own roses
Naturally

A brilliant
Blossom
Of yourself
Will never fade
Upon the shelf
A living rose
So beautiful to see
That you grew
The hard way
Naturally

Seasons pass
You'll want it fast
Comparisons distract
You'll tire of this song I sing
You'll tire of the fact

Then with a morning sunrise
A scene is sure to play
You'll turn to see
Your rose
Now a bouquet

Then to the young
Who turn to you
You'll say

Take the thorns
The heat and toil
The time to plant
And till your soil
This, my family recipe
For growing your own roses
Naturally
Growing your own roses
Naturally
Growing your own roses
Naturally

Chapter Seventeen

"The Snap"

It was now February, 1998. For the two years we were married, Alan and I had really tried. Again, there was so much love and shared music. But at this point we were living as roommates, politely tip-toeing around a big elephant in the living room, called "intimacy." "Intimacy" was starving to death and we did not have the tools as a couple to feed it. We did not fight and we did not make up. Something had to change. Someone had to move us toward our individual destinations and in my case, years and years of even more solo emotional work. So, out of love for us both, I blew a painful whistle loud and strong, strong enough to awaken Alan's possibilities and my own as well.

The night I knew I had to leave, I heard for the very first time what I now refer to as, "the snap." "The snap" is that moment when an ending, an ending that may break your heart, must take place. I heard that snap late at night while Alan slept. I walked around our dark apartment with my three cats watching, quietly taking an imaginary inventory of what I would take with me. That meant my handful of antiques, Barbara's paintings, the handed-down art, and the contents of the single armoire that Alan and I had built for me when I first moved in. It was no one's fault. We simply did not know how to build a union impossible to break, impossible to walk away from.

Of course it was not about running from Alan to another man. I was to face another long and humbling chapter alone. With only a bruised ego to partner, I would finally admit that for any man to be with me he must challenge my stoic walls that I put up to protect myself from being disappointed once I knew that I truly needed another person. My walls could hurt, neglect, patronize, and distance. In the decade following my time with Alan, week by week, and session by session, Lana and I would chip away at those walls.

Within two weeks of "the snap," I had packed up my few belongings and moved to Lynn's, where I would camp out on her couch for about three weeks. I would retrieve two of my three cats once I found a new home and leave dear Harriet with Alan. Although Alan and I cried beautiful tears, neither of us fought this decision. But it was terribly, terribly sad. There would be much to grieve, so much loss to process.

I am most proud of how we handled our separation and divorce. Since I truly believed in "growing my own roses," I was not to be supported by an ex-husband. You can't have it both ways. I simply asked Alan to help pay for my move and replace the few items I would need to create a new home that I could afford on my own.

After a couple weeks with Lynn, the rainy Saturday came when it was time for me to head out and find an apartment.

"I will not return until I have found a new home."

It was almost closing time when I walked into the real estate broker's humble store front on East 75th Street.

"What can you afford?"

"Under $1,000 a month."

"Take these keys and look at this one."

The broker was a transvestite who looked a great deal like Shirley Jones when she played the pop singing mother in the 70s sitcom, *The Partridge Family*. So, for this story I will call her Shirley. I took Shirley's key and climbed all six floors of an East 78th Street walk-up building of studio apartments. I climbed and climbed to the very top floor. I thought with each step that at least I would get into good shape living there. When I arrived at the top floor, I heard Annie Lennox sound from the apartment next door to the one that would be mine. The sounds of a shower splashing and the delicious smell of bath products foaming accompanied my unlocking of this mysterious door and my prayer that I would survive this move.

"I can make this a home, I can make this a home, I can make this a home," I said out loud as I walked down the tiny hallway that connected the main room, kitchen and bathroom that I would spend the next three years of my life in. I could make it a home, and I did make it a home. It was an extraordinary home, and one that I would later refer to as "the healing house."

When I heard the shower next door stop, I knocked on the door. A beautiful young brunette, dressed in a terry cloth robe opened the door. She was glorious as her freshly-showered skin lit up the dark corridor that connected our two apartments.

"Hi. I'm Meg. I am thinking of moving into the apartment next door. How is this building? Is it safe? Are you happy here?"

"Oh, yes. You will love it. Do it. Move in."

I listened to her and went back to Shirley who kept her office open late just for me, another city angel! I filled out the application and borrowed her enthusiasm as I made this spontaneous, huge commitment. Alan generously paid the first and last month's rent, for my new futon and the household items I needed to make this one room a home. Lynn and I toasted on far too much wine while *I can make this a home, I can make this a home, I can make this a home* played like a movie soundtrack in my mind throughout the week before moving day.

When I attended a cousin's wedding the following summer, one of my uncles said to me, "Good lord, Meg. By the time we all got home from your wedding, you were divorced."

"Yes, it's true."

But it was OK, as long as I was happy now. Well, I wasn't happy now. I wasn't sad either. I was alive with a great deal of work to do. The next couple of years would challenge and inspire me, starve and feed me, and ultimately replace my dated quest for "happiness" with the goal of growing a real woman of myself.

You see, I had no business being married to anyone yet. When I met Alan, I was just beginning to unravel and release the myths I had told myself thus far. Myths that seemed painted, carved like co-conspirators in to that heavy mask that successfully pushed away true emotions, true creativity and true love making. Like a scratch on a record that skips and skips and skips, preventing the song from finishing, I did it again. I stopped the work again. I ran in to the arms of yet another man and actually married him this time. My sister used to say, "You can run, but your grief will wait for you." My grief finally caught up with me.

Alan was a diamond, but he was not to be *my* diamond. We each played a key role in the other's evolution. I remember reading that some people can go life's distance with one partner, and some need a few tries. I clearly was the latter.

Alan attended my father's funeral six years after we separated. I will never forget the support I felt seeing his warm and moved face smile back at me as I stood and spoke of my father's life and legacy that December day. Ironically, our fathers shared the same birthday, May 24th. Alan was and is a class act. I am honored that I made music with him literally and figuratively as long as I did.

With a Snap

You've mastered pretending
Avoiding the ending
You can't ignore
You've been here before

This time can't run after
Clouds void of laughter
That tempt one more try
Like a hovering sky

With a snap
Brittle twig
Hear it echo
With a snap
Bitter pill
Can't deny what you know
These crumbs will not grow
Turn and go
With a snap
Turn and go

Butterflies dive inside
Hold on twisted ride
Till it's over for sure
As you slam the car door

Rewrite it
Don't fight it
Bear down
Stare down what's empty
To be free

With a snap
Brittle twig
Hear it echo

With a snap
Bitter pill
Can't deny what you know
These crumbs will not grow
Turn and go
With a snap
Turn and go

No mistaking
Awakening
The snap is the sound you are hearing
Every day
Chips away
Little deaths
Making room
For the clearing

The calm after the storm
Silent and warm
Take a seat
Await the next beat

It's like angels appear
Singing hymns in your ear
Divine sign
You did it this time

With a snap
Brittle twig
Hear it echo
With a snap
Bitter pill
Can't deny what you know
These crumbs will not grow
Turn and go
Turn and go

With a snap
Brittle twig
Hear it echo
With a snap
Bitter pill
Can't deny what you know
These crumbs will not grow
Turn and go
With a snap
Turn and go
Turn and go
Turn and go
With a snap

Chapter Eighteen

"It's About Time"

My parents were always amazed at how I could get things done. It was when they saw my mattress go out the front door in my sophomore year of college that they learned that I was moving out to share an apartment in Hell's Kitchen with an older dancer I had met in class. It was on moving day that they learned about my new apartment on East 78th Street, the place I would file for divorce and begin again.

On moving day, my parents showed up not quite sure what to expect from their daughter. They climbed the six flights of stairs to the top floor, where I was to spend the next three years of my life. Mom made a joke that she better make friends with someone living on the third floor to catch her breath the next time they visited.

I had everything mapped out perfectly. I have a gift of making a home out of any space that I live in. I learned this skill from Mom. No matter where we lived, no matter where we moved, she found a way to turn that space into a home that I would be so proud to bring my friends to see. While in the Peace Corps, we never knew what kind of military-like house was waiting for us on the other side of a long flight across the Pacific. Mom simply walked into the space, looked right, and then left, and then turned to Dad and said, "Take the kids somewhere and come back in a few hours." When we returned, she had made the space a home. Pictures were hung, pillows placed, bathrooms scrubbed, beds made, and familiar dolls, books, albums and even gerbils were put where we could see them upon our return. We were "home" in a country so very far away from home.

I inherited this gift, and I think I channel my anxiety this way. If I can make the externals orderly and clean, then maybe, just maybe, my internal life will follow suit. Once again I knew where to hang every framed piece of Filipino art, the portrait of my mother's namesake, and Barbara's original oil paintings. I drew little floor plans while riding the subways days before moving day, thinking through where the three antiques, two chairs and new futon would be put to transform the room with its stark, white walls, tiny kitchenette and short hall to a sea foam blue-tiled bathroom. This studio was bare and functional, and showed signs of being occupied and then left without a thought. It was like a one-night stand with a stranger one would never see again. The freshly painted walls and shiny wooden floors helped, but I could feel the many anonymous souls who did hard time within the four walls.

I bought white towels, a bath mat, and a shower curtain to give my sea foam bathroom a hotel-like feel. Along the hall I hung framed black and white photographs of myself as a baby and child, along with photos of grandparents, parents and siblings. I knew that I was going to do some serious looking backward into the past to piece together why I had made the choices I did. I was pretty darn lucky to get a second chance at love and I had better get it right this time.

However, Alan was kind and generous to me, and never abusive. If this union had taken place even a few decades ago, most women would have stayed. I got a second chance. Society had given me permission to want more for myself, but I knew not to squander this second chance. My issues had accounted for fifty percent of this marital failure, and I had better do some serious self-analysis to change my old tapes. The black and white photographs of my past seemed to play the overture and stand as the backdrop for this solo dance that I was now to perform.

So, Mom and Dad entered my immaculate nest to be seated on the futon that served as my bedroom, living and dining room furniture. They exhaled with great relief. Again, their number four child was an independent, problem solver who wouldn't move back home. In a month I had left Alan and found a temporary place to live. I had pounded the city streets to find an apartment that I could afford without their help.

My parents delighted in John and Patrick, who were helping me to hang pictures, unpack the kitchen and transform the bathroom with a snow fall of white accessories. With each of my apartment endeavors I've learned that bathrooms keep no secrets. A couple of fresh coats of paint will neutralize just about every other room, but you will meet the past lives of the occupants who came before you in the bathroom.

Thankfully, my parents noticed that I didn't have any lamps and that the sun was starting to set. They ventured down the six flights of stairs with a "We will be back!" In about an hour's time, two stunning wrought iron lamps with parchment shades climbed up the staircase. They bought me one tall lamp to stand in the corner and a desk lamp to sit upon the antique wash stand that would serve as my desk. I still cherish these lamps today, and they sit in my currant home like medals of Honor awarded after a bravely fought battle. Dad also picked up a huge bottle of white wine to toast this new beginning. John and Patrick noticed that not only did I lack a television set, but that I lacked a stereo also. Within minutes their spare boom box was thumping party music as we five toasted this bitter sweet event.

Again, I was reminded that life may test you, but it also hands you all the help you need to endure your tests. John and Patrick happened to live one block away. Of all the apartments in New York City, I happen to find one a block away from my old boss and his beautiful tall, blond partner. For the next three years, I would find comfort in the fact that they lived just one block away if I needed a pep talk or delicious glass of expensive wine. These boys had taste.

By about ten o'clock, everything was put away. All the boxes and wrapping paper were carried down to the garbage cans that lined the simple steps of the building. All my clothes were hung and the appliances put away in the three small closets that stood along the short hallway from the bathroom to the room where I would meet myself, again. An overwhelming deja vu came over me. It seemed to scold and humiliate me. I had been here before. I had been here before when Doug left. I had stood in an empty apartment faced with only my pattern of filling the empty space with a man. This round with Alan proved to be too expensive emotionally, physically, and financially for us both. Enough was enough. I had to get off this ride once and for all.

I slept pretty well that first night, but the tough day to follow came up quickly with the East side sun. Alan was going to deliver my two older cats and see my new apartment for the first time. When he walked through the door with the two cat carriers, he knew in a flash that I was not coming back. This was not a temporary separation. We were done and that was very, very sad.

Peanut and Thaitu roamed the small hall with body language that seemed to say, *Really, really? This is our home now?* But God bless them, they adjusted. Their lives had begun with wandering the city streets as abandoned kittens. I had never let them down so far. Once the litter box, water and food bowls were set in place, they quickly discovered where the ideal napping spots were on the new futon cover with matching pillows.

Alan was incredible. He knew that the perfectly unpacked and decorated space meant I was not coming back, but he filled the awkward silence with compliments. After we visited, I walked him to the Second Avenue bus and gave him a long hug. I said that he could call me anytime to talk and to process this new and odd transition. We loved each other so much and were such good friends. It was excruciating and it had to be.

I was earning my entire income as a commercial actress at this point. I had been very lucky the last few years, but it was naïve of me to think that I could depend on the casting whims of the advertising industry now that I was completely responsible for myself. I wasn't sharing expenses with Alan any longer, and I had to come up with a lot more money each month. I was determined to do this without any help, any help at all.

In retrospect, I am very proud of this fact. Sure, I wanted to run home to my parents every evening as the sun set. I dreaded those six flights of stairs to my box of an apartment, but I didn't run home. I climbed each step, unlocked the door, turned on the light to find my feline family, and chilled my Chardonnay wine.

However, the commercial business was changing and there was talk of a Screen Actors Guild strike. I was also very lonely. I missed my retail days of sisterhood, a structured schedule and a place to go during my "single in the city" nights and weekends. I was grieving my marriage and the outdoor cafes lined with couples in love with strollers and their golden retrievers were more than I could bear. I was in no shape to start dating. It was time to get a part-time job.

I could not go back to the large department store that I had worked for before marrying Alan. I had made quite a scene with my "So long girls!" exit that reeked of a certain "happily ever after" ending. To walk into the same store with my soon-to-be-divorced tail between my legs took guts, guts that I didn't have.

I remembered that a friend of mine had worked for a small, Swedish cosmetic company that had several shops in New York City. There was a location on Madison Avenue, just blocks from my new apartment. Lo and behold, when I walked in to simply inquire about a part-time job, they practically handed me a set of keys to close the shop up that night. They needed a free-lance makeup artist immediately, and I began the next day.

It's About Time

Been too many years looking over my shoulder
Thought it would change as I got older
Toning down what I say
Giving myself away
No more taking back what I mean
I'll scream when I want to scream
I want to scream

Time to practice what I've been preaching
While stretching out, my arms are reaching
On tippy toes into the air
I've swallowed truth
I'll swallow dare
No more apology for letting myself be
Please let me be

'Cause you see I've never been young
And I don't want to waste my prime
I've never been young
And I think it's about time
I think it's about time

Cut me loose of my puppet strings
And replace them with a pair of wings
'Cause I'm heading for the skies
Where no one buys my pack of lies
This invisible hold has gotten old
So very old

'Cause you see I've never been young
And I don't want to waste my prime
I've never been young
And I think it's about time
I think it's about time

Time to put the spark back in my eye
Time to give my heart another try
Time to laugh so hard until I cry
Time to fly

'Cause you see I've never been young
And I don't want to waste my prime
I've never been young
And I think it's about time
It's time
It's time

I think it's about time
It's time
It's time

I think it's about time

Chapter Nineteen

The sweetest Swedish!

This was the perfect fresh start. I was to sell cosmetics in a boutique this time, with white walls, matching marble floors and antiques. Instead of counters of glass, Formica and chrome, these testers were placed on vintage trays and mirrors, upon a huge, wooden dining room table. I was relieved by the manageable expectations and handful of rules to follow. The owners knew that I was overqualified and quite a bit older than the young beauties who bounced to the beat of Cher sounding from the shop stereo in their tight black tee shirts. I thought that it was a good sign that Cher blasted, "Do you believe in life after love, after love, after love?"

I could be anonymous now. I had no past to explain or a future to plan. I volunteered for the night and weekend shifts. I would do anything to avoid my empty apartment. Within days of the first shift, I mastered a nun-like existence in my new black tee shirt, walking to work with coffee in hand to open the store and a salad to go after closing.

My confidence began to grow. Since none of my co-workers had witnessed my past life, I was free to cut my hair even shorter, experiment with shadows, lipsticks and blushes that shimmered (these gals were big on shimmer), and follow the tight tee shirt lead of my new Swedish little sisters. The owners and management quietly knew that I was in transition and asked me few questions.

I've observed over the years that some performers were so ambitious, they would never allow anything to get in the way of their dreams, anything. When they got a "survival job" they refused to allow it to compete with their goal. They would call in sick if they couldn't change their shift for an audition and quit without notice if a last minute performance opportunity came their way. At this stage of the game, I was clearly the opposite. My "survival job" was becoming more than a means to supplement my commercial acting income and pay gig expenses. My shifts in the shop were feeling like a career, a brilliant career!

My agents began to sense that my passions were changing. I had made every appointment they arranged with enthusiasm, determined to support myself entirely as a commercial actress, but something funny started to happen. The phone would ring in the store with a, "Meg it is your agent." Once upon a time this would have thrilled me. It would define and justify me. I had worked for decades to be able to sign with such a reputable commercial agency. Every audition was a gift and fed my identity. Now I would be in the middle of a make-over, totally engaged in meeting my customer's needs, and dreading the possibility that I had to sneak out for a last-minute audition that afternoon. It was time to sit down and redefine my path.

I had made personal business cards that said, "Meg Flather—Real Makeup for Real People." I loved building a personal clientele of brides, actors in need of headshot artistry, and corporate big shots who could afford private applications in their home or office. The audition experience of reading scripts filled with words I would never say for products I would never use was beginning to feel like an obligation, rather than an opportunity. I still loved being on-camera, and I loved performing, but I wanted it to be on my terms, utilizing the confidence and power I felt when handing out one of my home-made business cards. I made an appointment to meet with all the agents, and proceeded to shock them.

They were sure that I had set up this meeting to complain, to grill them with, "Why was I not called for that audition, and why didn't you submit me for that job?" Instead, I laid out a new plan. Going forward, I would only attend auditions when I was specifically requested. There would be no more open calls playing "young mom," "young wife," or the poor man's fashion model, never to be hired, but put through the ringer of callbacks wearing nothing but a bathing suit, or like the time I actually stripped down to my bra.

It was an audition for a massaging shower head. The casting director had a group of us remove our tops and face the wall, which we all did without hesitation, wanting so much to please, so much to be cast, leaving all self care and self respect in the waiting room. While facing the wall, the sound of a portly advertising executive slurping a sandwich with far too much mayonnaise was finally interrupted by him asking me, "Are you aware that you have a colony of moles on your back?" That is when I heard a new "snap" and then answered with attitude, "No, I did not know I had a colony of moles on my back!"

So, it was time to combine my on-camera skills with my love of skin care and beauty sales. I instinctively knew that if I said no to one aspect of the business, making it clear what door I wished to open, the invisible world would hear me and take an active role.

Afterwards the agents complimented me on my mental health, saying that they had never had a client hold such a meeting. I walked out of the office no longer a commercial actress, but a partner in business. The beeper didn't go off like it used to, and the shop phone did not ring for me daily. However, when I did get an audition, the job reflected my skill set and I usually booked it. My acting income decreased, but my self-confidence soared.

Too Intense for You

You can look
But you can't touch
The pressure would be
Oh too much
Oh too much for you to bear
To hear her voice
Begin to care

'Cause that's the time
You'd up and run
'Cause you just wanted
Something fun
She's too intense
Too intense for you

She won't look you
In the eye
'Cause you're the type
To make her cry

She just keeps
Her shades in place
To never share
Her fragile face

'Cause that's the time
You'd up and run
'Cause you just wanted
Something fun
She's too intense
Too intense for you

She just might
Return your smile
And if you're smooth

She'll flirt awhile

But she'll know
When it's time to go
'Cause you won't try
To get to know

All the voices
In her head
And all the lives
That she has lead
And all her questions
Asking why?
Like who and what's beyond the skies?
Like who and what's beyond
Your eyes?
Your eyes?

She keeps her heart
Fixed on the goal
She stays aloof
And in control

To fight that hungry
Voice within
That longs for love
And lust and sin

'Cause that's the time
You'd up and run
'Cause you just wanted
Something fun
Something light
Fast and free
With no responsibility

That's the time

You'd up and run
'Cause you just wanted
Something fun
She's too intense
Too intense for you

She's too intense
Too intense for you
Too good for you?

Chapter Twenty

Mud

One day my beeper did go off. It was one of my agents with an interesting proposition. Apparently, a small skin care company with an even smaller budget was looking for a spokesperson to appear for them on a home shopping network at 6 a.m. for eight minutes, thank you very much. They didn't have the funds to hire a casting director and hold a real audition. Instead, anyone interested had to tape themselves selling a skin care product they loved. So, I got a friend to tape me selling an eye cream. I just adore eye creams. My childhood passion for cosmetics, Beverly's training, and those years before the commercial camera lens came together, and I got the job. It required me to prepare completely on my own and take a pay cut, but I knew this was the right next step for me.

OK, but here was the clinker—I was to sell mud. Mud from the mountains of Morocco that apparently draws out skin impurities if one leaves it on one's face long enough (but watch out for your white bathroom towels. What a mess!). This was going to be a tough sell, but it was a start. Mud or no mud, this was my introduction to the Wild West of cable shopping television, and I was on board 100%. Thankfully, this project was going to take some time to come to fruition. The mud people had to pitch their product to the channel and everyone involved had to agree on a kit, a price, and a launch date. While all this was going on, I was blowing up my life puzzle on my East side floor.

I was committed to Lana with even more intensity and focus. I was able to delve into all the facets of my story, now that I had nothing to lose. My going through a divorce just two years after a huge family wedding set me free in many ways. The cat was out of the bag. I was not perfect. I was not happy. All was not well. This newfound freedom allowed the therapy process to finally begin. With each session, I allowed Lana to guide me through darker and darker emotional hallways which I had resisted when I had felt "perfect," "happy" and "well." Lana's exquisite care and intuition were helping me become real, like the rabbit in the children's classic, *The Velveteen Rabbit*. Indeed, I was worn out and bruised, like the beloved, stuffed animal, but my exposed, faded coat and frayed whiskers reflected a truth which Lana insisted was beautiful to behold. I found this hard to believe, but kept going just the same. I borrowed Lana's will and certainty every step of the way.

As for my music, I was now working with a talented guitar player named Ben from Australia. He needed the work, and I needed to sing. We began performing my original songs on Sunday nights at the Dark Star, the downstairs venue of The Triad on West 72nd Street. The Sunday manager was another angel in my life. Whether I sang for an audience of five or fifty, he supported this endeavor. Together, we began to grow a real musical community. I would work my Sunday shift at the store and simply walked across the park for the sound check. Ben and I sat side by side on tall stools upon a platform that served as a stage. In between songs, I began to improvise and tell stories, unaware that I was practicing the unscripted exchange with an audience that my future career in television sales would demand. There are no coincidences! Ever!

After our set, I sat and savored the singers who followed me, sipping my complementary glass of Chardonnay. I was thankful for the musical community that the Sunday manager created for us all. Ben and I began writing songs and before I knew it, my second album, *It's About Time* was ready for recording.

As for men, I danced with a few. There were a few late night calls to my crush who was supportive, but who was also falling in love with his future wife. There was the younger man who found this sexually starved Mrs. Robinson intriguing for about five minutes and then there was Dan the actor.

Dan saw me sing at an open mike and then came to see my full set with Ben. He approached me after our set for my phone number, and I gave it to him. When he called me to ask me out, he insisted that we not meet for coffee (my suggestion), but go out for dinner. So it began. Dan wanted a girlfriend, and I was ready for a boyfriend.

Dan was intense, intelligent, and committed. He dove into our courtship with full throttle. He called when he said he would call, showed up when he said he would show up, and saved every Tuesday, Thursday, and week-end night for me. He made me and our growing bond the focus of his life. My abandonment issues made this a huge gift for me at the time.

However, Dan was in therapy too, and we proceeded to over-analyze just about every moment of our time together. Indeed we made love, but if we weren't examining everything about it, we were crying all the time. We had intense nights which caused me to go to work the next morning drained and confused. I started getting "in trouble," which worried my friends, especially Lynn. If I was five minutes late to telephone him or to meet him, it "hurt" him, and meant that I was not "present" to the relationship or his needs. By the time he broke up with me, I was emotionally exhausted. But his brave com-munication style and unwavering commitment did serve me.

Dan gave our time together everything he had, but late on a Monday night, I got the telephone call. He had just had a session with his therapist, and he realized that he "could not have all his pieces" with me. I told him to keep the coffee maker I had kept at his apartment, and I mailed him the CD he had left behind in mine. Dan called me a year later to re-connect. Instead of saying, "I miss you, Meg," He said, "I miss the me I was with you, Meg." That about says it all, don't you think?

But I will say this; I will never thank Dan enough for his support the day I finally did ride that Amtrak train bound to sell my mud. He would wake up early to watch my eight minute, 6 a.m. debut on home shopping and im-mediately fill my answering machine with affirming messages. I will always re-member the loving role he played on that big day.

Thank You

Am I allowed to be this happy?
With you standing there before me?
Arms open and eyes clear
I can't believe you're finally here
Just in the knick of time
Baby, you're mine

And I worked hard to arrive
To do much more than stay alive
And my darling, so have you
With all the roads you've sorted through
Oh, no more need to roam
Welcome home

So, what happens now?
We trust this place
We dare to bear
This foreign space
With no dramatic interlude
Instead be filled
With gratitude
Thank you
Thank you
Thank you

We'll swap the baggage in our hands
And we'll delve to understand
Where I've been or what you need
To follow or to lead
What tempo and what speed?
We'll find our speed

And I pledge to do my best
When facing the next test
I'll rise to see what's left in me

To set my demons free
Let's set those demons free

So, what happens now?
We trust this place
We dare to bear
This foreign space
With no dramatic interlude
Instead be filled
With gratitude
Thank you
Thank you
Thank you
Thank you
Thank you
Thank you

Am I allowed to be this happy?
With you standing there before me?
I better learn to be this happy
With you standing there before me
I'm gonna learn to be this happy
With you standing there before me

Chapter Twenty-one

Bitten by the bug!

As my car approached the entrance, my heart began to pound. I suddenly realized that the entire facility was the size of a small town! As my car rounded every corner of the long and winding entry road, I took great comfort in the beautiful, tall trees that lined each side of the road and extended back into what looked like an endless forest. These green leafy angels hovered above me, like the tall showgirls from my theatrical past who knew just when to give me an encouraging wink before it was my turn to perform a solo in front of a crowd of strangers.

When the car finally stopped, I walked up several flights of stairs beyond a circle of poles flaunting flags from countries the network broadcasted from. The receptionist gave me a name tag and instructed me to walk down the long, tiled corridor to where the selling magic would soon take place. I started walking and felt like I was instantly beamed up to a huge space ship. With each step, each new *click, click, click*, I felt my connection to civilization slip away. I had no sense of time, date, weather, or season. I had no connection to anything outside the studio doors of my destination. I was now in a huge selling bubble and was absolutely thrilled by this fact.

After I checked in at the production desk, I was instructed to wait in my small dressing room that was connected to the other dressing rooms, and the even larger Green Room. In the Green Room, other vendors and spokespeople were preparing to sell their products. They sat in large easy chairs and on sofas, sipping coffee while watching the huge television screen broadcasting what was happening live in that moment on television.

The Green Room had a wall of glass windows that looked out onto the set below. This way you could also watch from above what was being filmed that very moment. But, more importantly, there were computer screens on desks along the other Green Room walls, calculating the exact dollars being sold per minute for each product presented in that hour. Needless to say, it was this fact that overwhelmed me most of all.

I was used to pre-performance nerves. I knew how to recite lines or song lyrics in my head to steady my anxiety and make sure that I knew my part. I was used to saying to myself, *What if I forget my lines?* but not, *What if no one picks up the phone to buy my mud?* I was now to be evaluated on my DPM (dollars per minute), and I felt out of control. No matter how charming I was, how prepared I was, and how witty I was, if the ladies did not want my mud, I would not be back.

Thankfully, the consultants the mud people had hired to handle me were lovely and supportive. They distracted me from my nerves by reiterating how nice I looked (in my taupe meets cantaloupe, silk Tahari suit which I last wore on my wedding day), and kept saying how I "would do just great." Thanks to these ladies, I was pumped and ready to roll by show time.

It was soon my turn to sell. A nice gentleman put a microphone on my lapel and an earpierce in my ear. The earpiece was needed in case anyone in the control room needed to talk to me during the sell, or if a customer called the show live to ask me a question. This was new for me, but I could handle it. At least that is what I kept saying to myself.

A very attractive blond woman met me right before she went on to host the hour. In a matter of fact way, she jotted down my key selling points (the features and benefits of my product), and asked what questions she should ask me to focus my sell. She told me that I was to follow right after the segment on vacuum cleaners. I was escorted to the set where I would stand and wait for the host to come to me when the time came. In the distance I could hear the sale of the vacuum cleaner winding down. I thought, *What a gift? My mud draws out the impurities beneath the skin's surface like a vacuum cleaner sucks up dust and dirt from the floor. This could work!*

Now I was in heaven, I was on fire, and I was fearless. I had come home. I had found my new place. I hit all my points. I talked about the history of the mountains of Morocco, how for generations they were known for their age-defying mud, and how this rare mud draws out skin impurities, leaving the face silky smooth and younger looking. My metaphor comparing exfoliation to vacuuming floors went over really well. The host laughed, nodded, and seemed to really want me succeed. Even the poor model dressed in a terry cloth robe smiled at me from beneath the gobs of mud I applied to her face. However, in the end, none of that really mattered. The dollars per minute would define my future, and my dollars per minute were low. I didn't reach my sales goal.

But I was hooked. I had fallen in love with this Wild West of cable shopping television. I had to do this and I would do this. It would take me another few years before I found myself in front of this particular camera lens again, but I was determined that I would get there. I would get there. Indeed, my name was mud, but I was OK with that. I would make lemon aid out of my muddy 6 a.m. lemons, because I was certain that someday, I would return. Someday I would return.

Downstream

You can go ahead of me
I'm not in a hurry
I stood in line
I did my time
Of wanting
And of worry

I'm swimming downstream
I'm taking it slow
I'm swimming downstream
I'm watching the show

I'm swimming downstream
I'm taking it slow
I'm swimming downstream
I'm watching the show

Why the pace?
And why the race?
Where is the highway going?
Speeding kills
I'll get my thrills
Where tranquil
Water's flowing

I'm swimming downstream
I'm taking it slow
I'm swimming downstream
I'm watching the show

I'm swimming downstream
I'm taking it slow
I'm swimming downstream
I'm watching the show

Share a sunset
With waves that meet a shore
No more upset
From games of wanting more

Find the shadows
Leave behind
No evidence or trace
Let the young one
Talk to fill
This meditative place

'Cause I'm swimming downstream
I'm taking it slow
I'm swimming downstream
I'm watching the show

I'm swimming downstream
I'm taking it slow
I'm swimming downstream
I'm watching the show

Talk, talk, talk, talk
Let her talk, talk, talk, talk
While I'm swimming
Swimming downstream

Talk, talk, talk, talk
Let her talk, talk, talk, talk
'Cause I'm swimming
Swimming downstream

Chapter Twenty-two

Spokeswoman!

There I was living my small, manageable life on East 78th Street, working my retail cosmetic shifts, attending the occasional commercial audition, and making music weekly with Ben. The necessary time needed for my new creative seeds to grow had passed, and the signs that they were sprouting just in time for spring were apparent to me. Ben and I had about eight songs ready to record. Since my brief encounter with home shopping, I was fully committed to sharing my passion for cosmetics before a television camera. But how was that to manifest? I didn't know.

Again, the universe would play its funny game with me. Again, it would give me just what I needed to complete the next creative project, but not enough for me to grow too comfortable, fat and happy after the fact. I miraculously booked a commercial campaign that grew into a huge job which earned enough money to record my second album.

The commercial campaign was for the telephone and Internet provider of Rochester, New York. Like "the little engine that could" I am the queen of "the little job that could." This little, regional commercial ended up growing into a huge on-camera, radio and print campaign. The income I earned met the budget needs of *It's About Time*, with neither a penny more, nor a penny less.

Soon I learned that I would be alone for this creative chapter. The night before I was to fly to Rochester to shoot the first round of commercials, Dan asked me for space and did I mind if we "don't communicate" while I was away? Ouch!

I remember the makeup artist and wardrobe mistress watching me check my machine over and over again between takes from the dressing room pay phone. Their knowing faces smiled a smile that seemed to ask, "Really? This is acceptable to you?" Like the street smart and salty strippers in the final act of the musical, *Gypsy*, they knew what was best for this Gypsy Rose Lee Flather. They volunteered their own stories of men who could not share in their successes. Thankfully, Dan broke up with me two Monday nights later.

So with a heavy heart, I ventured to Astoria, Queens, several times a week, to record with Ben. My return to a convent-like existence was actually quite comforting. Once again I was getting far too much sleep, eating far too many healthy greens in an apartment that was far too clean, and giving my cats far too much attention. However, I look back on this summer with such gratitude. I loved this quiet, disciplined existence. It felt like I was back in school or camp. If I was not at work, practicing or recording, I was asleep. But another seed was beginning to sprout.

Seasons before the summer of 2000, a friend had suggested that I literally ask for what I wanted professionally. I placed my handwritten wish, my homemade business card, the jacket of my first CD, *Wake-up Call*, and a one dollar bill in a sealed envelope that I hid in my home. I tucked it deep in the inside drawer of the chest that stood in the middle of the little room that served as my dining room table, bedside table, music studio, client's makeup chair, and home office. This was my way of saying, "Please, please help me make total use of my skills as an on-camera spokesperson, a cosmetic consultant, and a singer/songwriter in the most complete way possible."

Lo and behold, fate responded that summer of 2000, but it took its own sweet time about it. I had to first let go of the theatre, commercial acting, the revolving door of men who did not love me and stand proudly upon the white tiled floors with my Swedish sisters, fueled by baked potatoes, cottage cheese, and apples. I had to be listening before the next gift was to materialize.

It turned out that my neighbor worked for a fancy public relations firm that handled the drug store brand, famous for the pink beauty fluid in a heavy glass bottle. Apparently, this "pink" brand had created a makeup line which was sold in mass stores with a makeup artist who loved color, but not the public. One night as I was unlocking my door with my "Real Makeup for Real People" kit strapped across my shoulder, my neighbor asked, "Hey, you are a makeup artist, right?" "Yes I am."

"Hey, I may have some work for you. Are you free Mother's Day?" "If you need me to be," and that was that.

The public relations firm had created a free make-over Mother's Day event in Rockefeller Plaza, and the celebrity makeup artist who created the line of shadows, blushes, lipsticks and nail enamels needed a second pair of hands. Lines of New York mothers, daughters and grandmothers waited for me to apply their cosmetics onto their faces and fill out cards of what makeup I used and how they could recreate their new look at home. All of my years managing gift events in a lab coat, applying eye cream in the mansion, and dusting glitter with my Swedish sisters came together in one day. I was fearless, I was eager, I was in heaven.

With each woman who sat in my chair, I channeled all that Beverly and the hours in stores had taught me. How to talk to a stranger, to make her feel comfortable, to meet her needs with colors to be sold, and to leave her with a positive feeling about the brand I was promoting. My neighbor's voice whispered in my ear, "Hey, they really like you. They have been watching you all day. Do you have a picture and a resume? There may be a job for you, Meg."

So, my picture and resume were sent to the corporate offices and an interview at the public relations firm was scheduled. When the lovely gentleman asked me about my makeup artistry strengths, my honest answer was music to his ears. I said something to the effect of, "After experimenting with cosmetics for years, my favorite job is to empower and build the self-esteem of real woman living real lives with affordable cosmetics that are easy to use on a daily basis. I actually started my own business. Here is my card." When I handed him the "Real Makeup for Real People" card, his face lit up and I knew I had the job.

On a side note, roughly two decades before all this, on the day that my grandmother died, I snuck in to her upstairs bathroom when the rest of the family was greeting guests and sipping tea. I opened the door to her medicine cabinet and next to her few bottles of prescription pills, dental floss, and Cover Girl pressed powder, was the same pink beauty fluid in the heavy glass bottle. I snuck that bottle in to my purse to keep a little of Nana with me. I held on to the bottle for years. It is pretty amazing that two decades later, I would go on to work for the company that sold that pink fluid. Nana must have been hovering during the interview, working her magic from above.

So, I was to be their National Spokesperson and Makeup Artist to work closely with public relations and marketing, and to promote the brand to real women, with real lives, on real budgets. Those who purchased this makeup from their local drug stores would read my tips in over fifteen fashion magazine articles, and later that year, would watch me as an expert in my field on a popular television talk show.

The television show featuring a male and female host who taped segments in front of a live studio audience, sharing gardening, cooking, interior design, fitness, finance, parenting and beauty tips. This is where I came in. I performed live makeovers on two audience members using only our latest color collection the first day, and using our age-defying skin care the next. The first day of shooting was a huge challenge when one understands that our latest color palette at the time featured purple and hot pink shimmery eye shadows. In my humble opinion, very few women can carry off purple and hot pink shimmery eye shadows.

There were no "Cover Girl" models planted in the studio audience to make my life easier. The producers selected "real" women for me to transform "live" on TV, and by golly, I did it. When the camera zoomed in close, these ordinary, but extraordinary ladies looked downright gorgeous, even in that purple and pink eye shadow! The secret wish I had placed in an envelope, in a chest drawer, in my box-like home was materializing right before my eyes on national television. The universe did come through for me. It did, but when it was good and ready, or better yet, when I was good and ready, or better yet, when I was finally listening.

Now something else was taking place at this turning point of the day. I was demonstrating a natural ability to banter with both hosts while blending those shadows, lining lips and selling my products. I was practicing the most important job requirement of my future home shopping career without even knowing it—allowing my host to lead our unscripted, conversational segment while I simultaneously created opportunities to share my prepared product's features and benefits, all within the legal limits of what the network required. How did I know how to do this? How indeed?

I flew home from this experience with video tapes of both segments that would play a huge part in my next home shopping booking. However, once again, I would have to wait years for this next opportunity to materialize. My ego would not be happy, but as the saying goes, "Better to be ready and never called than called and not ready." I get it. I have no choice but to get it.

Chapter Twenty-three

Dad's Castle

Everything was coming together. I was juggling my spokeswoman duties while recording my second album, and the Rochester commercial campaign continued. I had deposited all the commercial residuals into my savings account. I was growing a little nest egg and would soon need to invest it. Life in my six floor walk-up was comfortable, but the time had come to plant some adult roots. My East side rental was an anonymous and forgiving place to reinvent myself in, but it was time to find a new home and make use of the growing savings account.

Carolyn, (who I met fifteen years before while performing *Nine*) had fallen in love with a 1929, pre-war building, close to 10th Avenue. It was built as a residency for single women new to the city, and needing a safe haven to pursue their dreams. These women were actresses, dancers, writers and models. They were nurses, secretaries, executives and academics. Some were waiting to wed, and some would never marry. I could feel their spirits as I approached this brick fortress for the first time. I was charmed by the elevator operator, who stood like a palace guard in his cranberry red coat, to help me find my way to Carolyn's studio on the 15th floor. This fortress was comprised mainly of studio apartments, with only two one-bedroom apartments on each floor. It was very New York, very eccentric, very affordable, and very Meg.

Carolyn purchased her studio to serve her for the few days a week she came into the city to teach. It was a feminine little nest with two large closets, a kitchenette along the entry wall, and an adorable 1929 navy blue and white-tiled bathroom. Carolyn shook her finger at me and said, "For what you are paying in rent on the East side, you could own your own place here." Well, I

138

always did everything Carolyn told me to do. I called Dad and he agreed. "Time to pay yourself first, Margaret. Time to pay yourself first."

That same day, I told the doorman to give my name and number to anyone selling a studio in the building. Soon the phone began to ring. First there was a studio on the 5th floor, (too small). Then there was a studio on the 4th floor, (too expensive). Then there was a studio on the eleventh floor, (just right). This apartment had one of the largest studio layouts in the building. It needed a lot of work. The gentleman who had lived there apparently spent a great deal of money on his clothes, his women and on his car, but not a dime on his four walls. When Dad and I came to look at this "fixer upper," Dad reminded me of his real estate philosophy: that it is better to buy low and renovate a space yourself, than pay too much for someone else's taste and try to convince yourself you like it. "Buy right. Sell right, Margaret. Buy right, sell right."

Once again I was taken care of. I had to prove to Citibank Mortgage and the co-op board that I could afford the monthly mortgage, maintenance, electricity, gas, cable and phone payments that this new chapter would demand. Because of my spokesperson and commercial incomes, on paper I looked like a real success. Along with pages of application forms, I had to supply copies of pay stubs, tax returns and several letters of recommendation. Thankfully, my new boss, my agents and Carolyn's reference letters put the bankers' and shareholders' fears to rest. I was approved and purchased the apartment in the early spring of 2001.

Dad and I took the E train out to Home Depot to pick out light fixtures, ceiling fans, kitchen cabinets, sinks and faucets. I didn't realize at the time that the seeds of his cancer were taking hold, and in just three years he would be taken from us. When I think about the quality time we shared commuting to Queens, walking the aisles of Home Depot, and debating tile and paint chip shades, I am again so thankful. We made such a beautiful home together. On moving day, when all the boxes were unpacked and my two wrought iron lamps were put in their new spots, I asked Dad, "Do I really get to stay here? Do I really get to live in such a beautiful home?"

Imagine rich, red Italian floor tiles set against a sparkling white kitchen as you enter the apartment. In the main living space, imagine the original hard wood floors lovingly restored by a family of craftsmen who possess the uncanny gift of preserving the mystery of the past as they deliver the desired high gloss of the present. See oak shades hanging from each window that perfectly match the historic floors, soft taupe walls, and the three customized closets concealing all that I needed to store. Finally, imagine the same Italian floor tiles, set against a sparkling white bathroom, paralleling the kitchen entry and bringing the experience full circle. This is the one-room castle which Dad and I built together.

My three antiques, the portrait of Mom's namesake (who somehow knew to wear her brick red dress to match my Italian tiles one day), the Filipino prints, and Barbara's cloud paintings never looked so at home. All I had to purchase was a brand new futon cover with matching pillows to accentuate my new taupe walls and white ceilings. At the end of my city days, I would feel a warm embrace, Dad's embrace, as I unlocked both sets of locks to the door of the apartment. Our debates over fixtures, and Dad's pep talks demanding that I be more assertive with the contractor, shimmer like rare family jewels in my memory to this very day.

Just as I was feeling like a superstar spokesperson in her new superstar apartment, I learned that the makeup line I was representing was being discontinued so that the company could focus entirely on their new and improved skin care brand. They would be tapping the fifty year history of the famous pink beauty fluid, bringing it to the next century. So, if I were a dermatologist, they would be happy to find a new spokesperson role for me, but being a makeup artist, I was out of a job. Within weeks of moving day, it was time to pound the city pavements for work. I blew the dust off my retail resume, put a couple "Real Makeup for Real People" business cards in my wallet, and marched across Central Park to the last swanky department store I worked in before getting married.

This was no time for pride. The last time Rhonda had seen me I was singing, "So long girls", certain that marital bliss would save me from ever freelancing in a department store again. Rhonda was the Cosmetic Floor Manager. However, like the tested female ghosts who walked the halls of my 1929 fortress, Rhonda did not judge me. After she listened to my tale of getting married, divorced, living on the East side, working for the Swedish, getting the spokesperson job, losing the spokesperson job, my commercial money all spent on an apartment that I now could not afford, her response was simply, "Yes, Meg I think I have something for you." Again, there are no shortages of angels in New York City. One just has to remember that they come in all sizes, shapes, and colors, and in Rhonda's case, quite fashionably dressed.

I had got myself into my brick fortress as a spokesperson. The powers that be didn't need to know that now I was freelancing again to pay my bills, making roughly twenty dollars an hour. I was back on a budget, "growing my own roses," living on baked potatoes, cottage cheese, and apples. But I could handle this slight change of plans. I had Dad's warm embrace of a castle to wake up and come home to.

Grace

Distractions
Filled my day
My mind, my mood
To make this go away

Predictions
Promised more
To help me cope
And count on distant doors

I look for grace
In the face of this
Empty space
I look for grace
In the face
Of this empty space

I am ordinary
In imperfect skin
Free the load I carry
In this place I'm in

Holding what I need
In empty hands
To grow where planted
To land where I land

I look for grace
In the face of this
Empty space
I look for grace
In the face
Of this empty space

No more searching for rainbow's end
Private parties and fair weather friends
Look at life through a different lens

Take the road less traveled
Bear how it bends

I look for grace
In the face of this
Empty space

It's not up to me
I don't own what's mine
I trust what I can't see
Without a sign

I got the changing weather
This sweaty brow
All I'm feeling
In this moment now

I look for grace
In the face of this
Empty space
I look for grace
In the face
Of this empty space

I look for grace
In the face of this
Empty space
I look for grace
In the face
Of this empty space

I feel the grace
In empty space
I feel the grace

Chapter Twenty-four

The Pharmacy

On the morning of September 11th, 2001, I was getting ready to fly to Boston to appear in a regional commercial. My agent called me to turn on the news. We watched the local report, thinking that a stupid, inexperienced pilot flew his private plane into the tower and hoped no one was hurt because of his foolishness. This banter went on until the second plane flew into the second tower. After a long pause, my agent said, "Meg, you're not going to Boston today." We sat in silence, watching our individual television screens, knowing in that moment New York City, the country, and the world had changed forever.

My brother, Roger, worked downtown in the World Financial Center, just yards away from the Twin Towers. I kept calling Dad to see if he had heard anything from Rog. Dad refused to join me in my fear, panic, and hysteria. Dad always knew to counteract whatever drama was taking place around him with a calm and cool manner, almost devoid of feeling. At first, he would come across as uncaring, but I see now that his own emotional survival mechanism was at work. He knew that we both could not panic. That would make this tragedy all too real. One of us had to be calm. One of us had to deny it somewhat. So, his saying, "Don't go there, Margaret. Don't go there. I am sure he is just fine," was his way of holding on tight to innocence, security, I don't know, something that we all lost forever with the attack.

Thankfully, Roger was fine. He walked all the way up the West Side Highway first to see Dad, then to see each sibling, and finally to knock on my apartment front door. Of course Mom volunteered to work a double shift at the hospital. Roger's beautiful navy blue suit was covered with dust, and his face was pale. His inviting dark brown eyes were replaced by vacant, trauma-tized pools of exhaustion, but he was alive. He was alive when so many were not. When I opened the door, I rejoiced with relieved tears running down my face. However, within minutes my celebration turned into a paradoxical feeling of guilt. Why was my brother spared when thousands of innocent strangers perished?

Like Dad, I tried to suppress the evidence that this event affected me at all. My post-traumatic stress manifested in a subtle, hard to detect way. The weeks following that horrific day, I didn't talk about it, and I didn't cry about it, but I had the hardest time leaving the apartment, let alone the neighborhood. My usual get on and off the bus and subway self was stolen by the hijackers and replaced by a recluse. Just walking to the supermarket a few blocks away, was a huge undertaking. I could only stay tucked in my castle, absorbing the warmth and comfort from the historic wood floors and the handed-down art-work that had hung in almost every family home I had lived in. I could stay in the past for a few minutes if I concentrated hard enough. I could pretend it was September 10th.

My East side survival job was just too far away. The weekend after the attack, I called in sick. I could not get out of bed and stayed in bed that whole Saturday. However, I wasn't sick at all and used the time to write a song. I called Dad every hour or so to share the latest lyric, and to get his help with the last line of the last verse.

"Dad, I have 'Red, white and blue, da da da da.' I don't have that part yet, Dad, but I have, 'Unite a town of every shade and point of view.'" Within seconds, Dad came up with, "Three colors true. 'Red, white and blue, three colors true, unite a town of every shade and point of view.'"

As I recall this part of my story, I discover for the first time what a role Dad played in my 9/11 experience. While he was alive, we never addressed how we witnessed and processed the event together. Through the many calls about Roger, and the calls to share my song lyrics, and the completion of my one-room castle, Dad kept me safe. He gave me permission to panic, to process, and to hide as long as I needed to hide. How I wished I had shared this realization with him then. Well, maybe I just did.

The company Rhonda hooked me up to freelance for, somehow learned that I went to Boston to film the commercial that was originally sched-uled to film on 9/11 rather than work my shift. When I called to get my hours the following week, they did not put me on the schedule again.

Weeks later when I told my friend, Melinda, that I was out of work, she suggested we meet for coffee.

I had met Melinda at a mutual friend's wedding back in the early 1990s and we were reunited at the same friend's baby shower just a few years later. As the other mothers were engrossed in opening baby gifts, Melinda and I had escaped with a bottle of white wine into the empty dining room to medicate our lack of a husband and baby boredom. Melinda was fresh from completing years of an Ivy League education, but like me, she was now focused on exploring her inner life.

She was doing the same work with her therapist that I was doing with Lana, taking a hard look at the past to change the patterns of the present. Melinda was impeccably dressed in a soft coral suit. Her quick wit and brilliant mind reflected from her attentive and forgiving blue eyes. She was real, very much there, and so very safe to tell the truth to. We exchanged numbers and began our ritual of meeting for drinks which we both depend on to this day. Melinda's smile also began to consistently appear in my half-filled audiences when I performed my original music. In a language somewhere, Melinda must stand for "unconditionally loving friend."

Back to our coffee, Melinda's husband was taking over his father's pharmacy located on the corner of Broadway and 88th Street. Would I consider working for her for twenty-five hours a week? I could still go on auditions and interviews and focus on my music. In addition to my duties selling, she asked if I could help her purchase new skin care lines to fill up the crisp new shelves she just ordered. Could I decorate the front windows as I wished, reflecting each season, holiday or whim that came to mind? Could I also do my best to improve employee morale and customer service standards, tapping into my Beverly training? The answer was "Yes, yes, yes."

The pharmacy paid me just enough money to meet all my new expenses and provided a safe, family-owned haven for me after the world changed forever on the morning of September 11th. Without my knowing it yet, it would give me hours of practice for the breakthrough audition that would launch my home shopping career once and for all. The title of my 9/11 song was "To Begin," and the pharmacy was the ideal place to do just that, to begin.

To Begin

No matter where
I stood on the island
I could look over a shoulder
To find them
Please navigate
I'm running late
Guide me where
My city dreams prepare
Now nothing's there

I look for signs
Of a waking city
You raise the blinds
I'll make the coffee
Each little step
Is a start
To repair, rebuild
This broken heart

I sat by candlelight
I watched the heroes fight
I sang the vigil prayers
I passed the vacant stares
And they tell me darkness wins
If we don't begin

When the children ask
The many questions why
Amidst the late night tears
They're sure to cry
Let's choose the joy
Let's be of use
That's the way we'll win
That's the way they'll lose

In a flash
In a flame
Bloody steel
Buried shame
In a flash
In a flame
Bloody steel
Buried shame
Built to stand
Brave and tall
Watch them fall
We are kneeling
On the island
Feeling small

We sat by candlelight
We watched the heroes fight
We sang the vigil prayers
We passed the vacant stares
And they tell us darkness wins
If we don't begin

No matter where I stand
On the island
I now look over a shoulder
To find them
Red, white and blue
Three colors true
Unite a town of every shade and point of view
Red, white and blue
Three colors true
Unite a town of every shade and point of view

We sat by candlelight
We watched the heroes fight
We sang the vigil prayers
We passed the vacant stares

We sat by candlelight
We watched the heroes fight
We sang the vigil prayers
We passed the vacant stares

And they tell us darkness wins
If we don't begin
Time to begin

I'll make the coffee
You raise the blinds
Every little step
Every little step
Is a start

It's time to begin
It's time to begin

Chapter Twenty-five

"Sell me this hand cream."

So, when the world changed, the economy changed. My spokesperson job had come to me in the most magical way, through my neighbor arranging that one day of freelance work. How was the next big break to come my way? I had already made it very clear to my agents that I did not want to run around town auditioning for television and radio work unless I was specifically requested to do so. Although I could fill up the empty hours doing just that, I knew that I would be met halfway if I would take a new leap of faith. My new leap of faith was to simply show up—show up for the pharmacy, my song writing, and my intimate circle of soul mates. My life was small. My life was not impressive to strangers. My life was beautiful.

There was something so freeing about working in a pharmacy and not a high-end department store. I felt courageous as I watched others race to grab some kind of professional brass ring. When I would attend the few auditions scheduled for me, I was amazed how the dynamic in the room changed when I told the truth. When I fought the temptation to exaggerate how well my career was going with, "I am working in a pharmacy on the West Side part time" in an instant, the competitive, nervous tension in the room dissolved. "I love pharmacies, Meg! How cool is that?" and then without fail, that actor would pull me aside to confide in me about their lack of work, lack of opportunity, lack of direction. "How do we re-define ourselves, Meg, how?"

My simple existence was my leap of faith, my payment for what I knew was coming. Some seed was growing somewhere and would materialize when I was ready. I completely trusted this fact. Because of the 9/11 tragedy, New York City was given permission by the world to grieve. I gave myself permission to exist. What is that saying? "God laughs as men make plans?"

The second gift in this chapter was the reminder that belonging to a community helps remedy a broken heart. My pharmacy shifts rescued me from my sleeping, 9/11, post-traumatic stress and tendency to isolate. By joining the pharmacy family I immediately was embraced by an Upper West Side community of customers and a staff of four men. For the first time in my sales career I was surrounded by only men. There was the pharmacist, the cashier, the delivery boy and Frank.

Frank worked the front of the store, selling the hard milled soaps, perfumes, candles and stationary. He knew just about every customer's life story, let alone their names. Frank wore corduroy pants, cashmere sweater vests that perfectly matched his bold bow ties. In the movie of my life, Henry Fonda would sail back to earth to embody Frank's spunk and vigor. Frank was widowed and refused to stop working once he retired from a successful career in the garment industry. A few years before I was to meet him, he answered the ad for a part-time salesman. Luckily for me, he was to train and manage this new "holiday help" who would go on to work those "holiday" hours for the next two years.

Frank loved the theatre, film, a good novel, macaroni salad for lunch and a martini with just a few crackers with cheese for dinner. Again, a teacher appeared and this student was ready. When the store was quiet, Frank would recount every detail witnessing the great Gwen Verdon, Ethel Merman, and Mary Martin as they created their legendary Broadway roles on stage. We would blast the original Broadway soundtracks as we unpacked inventory to stock the shelves. Frank was in his late seventies and had more energy than all of us put together. You could always count on a curious look from him when you needed the "break" he never required.

I was thoroughly humbled by his effect on every individual who entered the store. Women of every age were charmed by his humor and touched by his sincere inquiries about their lives. He knew their husband's names, their children's names, their dogs and cat's names. He knew where they just vacationed and what flavor cough syrup worked for their youngest the last time she was sick with a cold. Frank was the master, old school salesman. He would only close the sale after a stimulating conversation was enjoyed and allowed that customer only to purchase what she needed. If we did not have what she wanted, he went out of his way to order what she wanted with a, "I will have it gift wrapped and delivered when it arrives, free of charge, Dear." Just about everyone was younger than Frank, so everyone was "Dear." When they were older, they still were called, "Dear." In this fragile time following 9/11 where I found myself questioning the integrity, the honesty of all institutions, I was blessed to soak in this man with such a standard, this mentor, this delightful flirt.

When Frank insisted on treating me to dinner, fellow patrons would warm our table with a knowing smile as they passed looking for the restroom, coat check or exit. There was something refreshing about this distinguished gentleman with a martini sitting across the table from a date, his daughter's age. This "lady friend" with her Chardonnay could not get enough of his life story. Frank grew up in Brooklyn, joined the army, fell in love, married, raised a family, and lost his love to cancer. Luckily for me his plan was to spend his remaining time on earth at the pharmacy. (When it ultimately closed in 2005, he went on to work at wine shop just a few blocks away. No retirement plans for Frank, no way.)

As I took pride tapping my cosmetic past, insisting my shoppers cleanse, exfoliate and moisturize their faces, Frank took care of their bath and body needs. He was responsible for purchasing all the body product lines and the beautifully wrapped, European hard milled soaps that lined the top shelves, just right of the cash register counter.

Now, I never cared about bath products. Mom and Dad had us all share the same bar of Dial soap, tube of Prell shampoo and bottle of Tame conditioner. Our thrifty, New England childhoods had no time for lounging in a tub of bubbles. If your hands were dry, you were out of luck. You dealt with it. But there I was inspired by Frank, ready to compete with him just a little and "move" this body care inventory too. Slowly I began to master the craft. "While you wait for your prescription, let me give you a hand massage with this delicious new lavender hand cream. Oh, do you smell that? Just like true lavender fields, so calming. Wow, look at how soft your hands have become in just seconds." SOLD! Just like that.

Here is where things get really magical. I had told my agents to only send me out on auditions I was right for. An Italian company was looking for a spokesperson to launch their bath and body line on Canadian home shopping television. What do you think I heard as the cameras rolled at the callback audition? "OK, Meg, sell me this hand cream." (Piece of cake.)
Thank you, Melinda. Thank you, Frank. Thank you, Upper West Side.

Middle Ground

Sitting in a lovely shade
Of charcoal gray
Rounding off the edges
For a new day, hey

Loving this lazy
Limbo I have found
I stare into the space
Let the quiet surround

I want to stop my pendulum swings
Between hot and cold
Don't want to surf my sea of extremes
A new way unfolds
Middle ground
Your center will hold
Middle ground
Your center will hold

Felt no pulse in my past
Unless dramas were played
I wouldn't go to embrace
'Till it drifted away

How do I walk the straight line?
Tune out the applause?
Don't want to read the reviews
Then clean up the flaws

I want to stop my pendulum swings
Between hot and cold
Don't want to surf my sea of extremes
A new way unfolds
Middle ground
Your center will hold

Middle ground
Your center will hold
Your center will hold

The second hand ticks
The moments expand
Stop spinning to fill them
With fantasies grand
I gotta bear what's before me
The truth on the wall
The cracks on the ceiling
My life that is small

I want to stop my pendulum swings
Between hot and cold
Don't want to surf my sea of extremes
A new way unfolds
Middle ground
Your center will hold
Middle ground
Your center will hold
Middle ground
Your center will hold
Your center will hold

Chapter Twenty-six

Honey!

The job was to fly to Toronto every six to eight weeks to promote Italian bath and body products on the only shopping channel in Canada. I knew nothing about the beloved family owned Italian company that had been in the skin business for over seventy years. I must have passed displays of their product line while working in my lab coat sixteen years before. I seem to remember beautifully wrapped gift sets featuring their honey line, warming the shelves by the escalators during the Christmas rush.

What was so spooky is Carolyn had just knocked on my studio apartment door to give me a complimentary body cleansing sample from the very quaint ocean side B&B she had just enjoyed with her husband. Before I tucked the sample away in my travel bag I remember thinking how refreshing the old world packaging was with its powder blue and white design, reminiscent of a much simpler, sweeter time. When I unscrewed the tiny plastic top to take in what was inside, the most intoxicating, decadent scent instantly served as a very much needed "time out" from the post 9/11 chapter I was still navigating. Well, who created that sample? These Italians! What was the flavor? White Almond! What would be Canada's favorite "flavor" once I launched the line months later.

So, when I put this all together I knew I had to focus 100% on this audition, giving it my all. I first went on line to the company website to read all about their history. I learned that they began as a leading pharmaceutical house, specializing in the cultivation of medicinal plants. That they soon realized that many of those same medicinal plant extracts offered skin amazing beauty benefit and soon found themselves in the cosmetic industry by accident.

Their home base was located at the foot of the Alps near Turin, Italy. Pictures and pictures of their 150 acres of botanical gardens, fields, cows and honey bees amazed me.

About a decade before this point, Sal, the main spokesman, introduced the company to American home shopping television and when this business grew, his elegant mother, Angela joined him on air. The demands for their US business were too taxing to manage a second account. So, the plan was to cast, train, and introduce a new "talent" to represent the brand with Sal and Angela for the launch and only for the launch. If the Canadian audience embraced this "talent" she would then sign a year-long contract, making a full commitment to the Italians and the channel as their on-air spokesperson. OK, now I was getting excited.

As I scrolled down the images on their website of all the bottles and bottles of cream baths, jars and jars of body creams and the tubes and tubes of hand creams, I began to talk to dear Frank in my mind. "Oh, Frank, now I will make you proud!"

Before the audition I went downtown to investigate their Soho shop. I sampled the delicious creams and "shopped" the store manager, observing her selling talents. She sent me home with literature about the products and as I rode the R train up town, I began to have that same, witchy feeling. This job was to be mine. This job was to be mine. As I read the literature I learned that the creators never used insecticides or pesticides when cultivating their plant extracts. I learned that they never tested their formulations on animals. That they do their best to match the scent of a living flower when creating their Lavender, Honeysuckle, Pink Peony and Lily of the Valley famous floral formulas. The casting director had a simple script for us to review before the audition, but I knew I had to do more to show this crew what I had to offer. So, I stayed up late the night before the first audition, tweaking, rewriting my script, in hopes of showcasing my years and years of experience standing in just about every cosmetic department in Manhattan. I had to show them I could communicate what skin needs, how this brand would meet those needs, while simultaneously creating a delicious aroma-therapy experience of the mind, mood and spirit.

The day came. I was rested, rehearsed and ready to do all I could to grab this bath and body brass ring. Even the casting director let his guard down after my audition was taped. He said something to the affect of, "Well, Meg, if this is not your job I will be shocked, shocked. Now, listen, though, the callbacks are taking place in the late fall sometime. They are seeing a lot of girls between now and then. A lot of girls. So, don't get discouraged if you don't hear from me for awhile. You will hear from me."

I flew home on invisible wings of bath bubbles. I had done my very best, my very, very best. Again, that great saying, "It is a tragedy to be ready and never called, but even more of a tragedy to be called and not ready" was sounding in my mind. When I was called, I was ready. I made sure of that and was on fire approaching my brick fortress that night. But now I had to wait and see what the Italians had in mind. Could they get past the name Flather? Could they trust their Mediterranean potions to a gal from Massachusetts who had not one drop, not one drop of Italian blood running through her limbs? Now, that was the question.

My Heaven (A Song for Bonnie)

I over hear them talk about tomorrow
Teaching one another how to pray
For shiny pearly gates aligned with angels
Certain that the sky will show the way

But I just passed a stranger on the sidewalk
Facing the same gritty, city day
Who with a random act of kindness
Made me want to stay

They pour the coffee
Drive the taxi
They guide the tired home and up a stair
Wearing wings and halos on the subway
My heaven's there
My heaven's there

When swallowed by the sound of my complaining
Sleeping through the meaning of this song
A stranger like I passed upon the sidewalk
Knows to pull me back where I belong

They pour the coffee
Drive the taxi
They guide the tired home and up a stair
Wearing wings and halos on the subway
My heaven's there
My heaven's there

My heaven's there
My heaven's there
My heaven's there

I over hear them talk about tomorrow
Teaching one another how to pray

For shiny pearly gates aligned with angels
Perhaps there more an urban shade of gray

They pour the coffee
Drive the taxi
They guide the tired home and up a stair
Wearing wings and halos on the subway
My heaven's there
My heaven's there
My heaven's there
My heaven's there

Chapter Twenty-seven

"But I will be in Australia that week!"

Now, we must rewind our story for just a bit, back to September 2000, a good two years before the audition roller coaster began. I was living in my East Side healing house, recording the *It's About Time* album and thriving in my spokesperson position. Again, I was getting far too much rest in an apartment far too neat, adding Cliff Bars and grilled chicken salads to my usual baked potatoes, cottage cheese and apple diet. Ben knew that if I was not recording with him, I was home alone with just my two cats. He knew it was time, it was "about time" I get out there.

Ben was working with another artist who was giving a rooftop party the Sunday after Labor Day. Ben insisted I go, insisted. I remember that Sunday morning. I stood in front of my closet shaking, fully certain I was going to meet someone at that party. *I don't need a man! I don't need a man! I am fine! I am doing just fine!* So, was I to wear the "Stay away from me overalls" or feminine, "come hither" ensemble? Although a good part of me was kicking and screaming, I chose the feminine, "come hither" ensemble.

The party was in Tudor City, that city within the city that peaks out at the East River, right by the UN. The apartment was on the top floor, with a beautiful roof deck. It was early afternoon and although I was wearing my "come hither" ensemble, my dark sunglasses and deep brown-red lipstick were sending the opposite message. *I don't need a man. I don't want a man. I don't need a man. I don't want a man.* Then I spotted Ben standing next to a fierce, warrior of a man. "Hey, Meg, this is my friend from Australia. He just moved here from Sydney."

This 6'4" tree of a man had the rosiest glow of a complexion. His silvery hair cropped close to his scalp seemed to capture the sunlight, creating a glow about him. Each line on his face carved a map of sorts, taking me (and just me) on a mini voyage to his past. Each line told a story of a risk taken and a lesson learned. His paradoxical blue eyes were as warm and comforting as they were fiery and bold. They confused me, challenged me, and delighted me. His feet anchored him as he towered above all the other guests, physically, emotionally, and intellectually. Jay was the most authentic and masculine man I had ever met. With my sunglasses and "stay away" lipstick doing everything they could to push him away, I knew, damn it, I knew, he was the one.

When Ben found his way to another guest, Jay did not begin the predictable, rehearsed monologue I was used to enduring when meeting a new man. Instead of the "Bla, bla, bla" resume this and that, he simply said, "I understand you are an image consultant. What should I be wearing to work?"

Wow! This was new.

"OK, well, I have always liked men in charcoal gray suits, crisp white dress shirts, black shoes that match the leather of their belt and watch strap and a tie with bright colors to complete the picture."

He went on to tell me he had a gray suit, the white dress shirts, the black leather shoes, belt and watch strap and several colorful ties. As this comfortable, easy banter continued, I became keenly aware that I was smitten. I was smitten.

He had been a musician for many years in Sydney, but as the business began to change, being a bit of a visionary, he knew it was time to shake things up and go back to school. He was accepted into an esteemed university and completed a rigorous degree in finance with two majors, no less. He moved to NYC to work for an accounting firm and to complete his first text book. This was a smart man, a very smart man who was also so very easy to stand next to.

What proceeded to take place was quite interesting. We were rarely alone at this party. Strangers kept coming up to us to chat as they munched on their potato chips with onion dip. One couple began asking me personal questions about my life like why my marriage failed. I decided to let it rip and test Jay still standing beside me. I answered every inappropriate question in detail and he was not fazed. He just stood there, tall as a tree, taking in my story, my intensity, all things Meg. As the sun set, he and Ben were ready to leave. We exchanged cards and off he went into the Tudor City sunset.

The next day I was so depressed. I just knew I had scared him away. I just knew it. I was too much, too much. Why did I do that? Why did I answer all those questions? I must have come across like a talk show guest on crack. I took the train out to Brooklyn to see dear Barbara and play with her sweet baby boy, Lucas. As I lamented on her futon sofa, she simply said, "Check your answering machine, Meg. Just check it." Lo and behold there was a message from him. A message from a man the next day. Rather than the hunting game where men don't call until Wednesday to make a plan for a Saturday, Jay called. Jay played no games. "Hello. We met at the party yesterday. I was wondering if you would like to go hear Ben play downtown Friday night. Give it a look?" Give it a look? Give it a look? I played the message for Barbara and even she was certain something very special and new had just taken place. Her Meg's life was about to change forever. Soon her Meg would get little sleep in an apartment filled with books.

That night I called him back to make our plan and so began a courtship unlike any courtship I had experienced before. He was my friend. We would share our passion for music, film, news, Indian, Japanese, Greek and Thai cuisine. He would cheer my performances as I launched my *It's About Time* CD, and I would keep myself busy watching his television as he completed his book from the kitchen table. Friends and family would not meet him for months. Although this slow down was very frustrating for me at first, Lana would explain how it benefited me most of all. I could finally give myself the time to truly get to know a man, all of a man before expressing my love and committing my heart. Lana would say, "It takes six months to love someone, Meg, six months."

Well, wouldn't you know it that the six month deadline fell on Jay's birthday? What came next illustrates just how perceptive, just how intuitive he was and is to this day. We agreed to meet for steak downtown. Jay was seated at the bar, eager, eyes sparkling and truly happy to see me. He was early to meet me (he is always early, never late for any appointment!) and was chatting up a storm as only he could with the bartender who said, "Oh, he was just telling me about you." Well, that felt nice. Something had shifted. What was it? Something was different. By golly, Jay was acting like a boyfriend!

Soon we were escorted to a private table in the corner of the restaurant, away from the festive merrymaking taking place at the bar. A formally dressed waiter helped seat me, gracefully scooting my chair to meet the crisp white linens and perfectly set silverware. Just as I was wrapping my purse around my knees under the table (I had mastered this by now!), Jay proposed to me. Right then and there, in his own "five sentences or less" succinct way, he proposed to me. I never became his girlfriend. I was fast-forwarded to fiancé between the complimentary cucumber salad and filet mignon. By fall, 2002, we planned my first voyage to Australia to meet all his friends, his "Mum" and to try on the family ring that had been saved in the top dresser drawer for generations.

After all the airline tickets were purchased, hotel reservations and cat sitting preparations made, and family and friends all scheduled to meet this Meg from New York, I learned that my callback audition was scheduled for the week I was to meet his mother. Once upon a time I would have rushed to cancel, cut short and deprive myself of this abundant voyage. This journey of new sights, tastes and loved ones whose delightful accents would almost sing my name. But the Meg with Jay was changed forever. I somehow knew, finally, to say, "No." If these Italians are smart, they will wait for me. They will have their callback auditions as planned, but wait to make their decision until they met this bride to be. This bride to be who would attend the final audition wearing the100-year old engagement ring from 10,000 miles across the Pacific that felt so at home on her hand. She would tell friends she swore it was waiting all those years in its faded, velvet box just for her. Just for her. Just for me.

His Ring

This ring
From across the sea
Tells the story
Of his family

The others who
Wore it too
Loved the land
The diamond sand
And the cockatoo

And I wear his ring
As I join the past
History
Carry me
To a love that lasts
I climb aboard
I take the ride
Silver band
Extend your hand
As a guide

So I can hear
Through a harbor breeze
The Red Coat lies
The tears and cries
Of Aborigines

The British naves
Leaving nameless graves
With chains and locks
They cleared the rocks
And paved the way

To wear his ring

To join the past
History
Carry me
To a love that lasts
I climb aboard
I take the ride
Silver band
Extend your hand
As a guide

Weathered ladies
Share with me
Tell me tales
Over pots of tea
Let's take some shade
'Neath the old gum tree

This ring
From across the sea
Tells the story
Of his family

The others who
Wore it too
Loved the land
The diamond sand
And the cockatoo

The sandstone high
It cuts the sky
The tribal lore
The stolen shore
The salty reefs
And eucalyptus leaves

And the kangaroo

Chapter Twenty-eight

"Maybe if we call her Margaret?"

On the day the audition was supposed to take place, Jay and I were flying from Sydney to Canberra to meet Mum and officially get engaged. In his classic style, instead of the violins and candlelight, down on one knee tradition, Jay and his mother simply stood by the kitchen table with sweet anticipation in their eyes. As I entered wearing his mother's bathrobe, very much in need of my morning coffee, he basically said, "Mum and I have something for you." Then a faded velvet box resting in his hand, hidden behind his back was placed in mine. I opened it to find a sturdy band with three, small diamonds that had solidified a century of marital unions and yet looked custom-made for me. The answer was, "Yes, yes I will marry you" and next I called Mom and Dad to share the great news. When I asked if the woman who last wore this ring was happy, fulfilled, in love with her husband to the end, his mother, sharing his practical, unsentimental wit replied, "Well, it was quite sad actually. She died of gangrene. She was a wonderful quilter, though, wonderful, great with the needle." After we all had a good laugh, I learned that this relative was happily married, and I hoped to channel some of her marital advice as I placed the ring on my finger for the very first time.

When I reflect upon my childhood which demanded so much show from me, my sprinkling of emotional saccharine to hopefully brighten up the never-acknowledged anxiety and depression in our home, there was something so right about how this authentic pair asked me to partner with them. I had always craved a real family around a real kitchen table and ended up finding just that as far away from home as a girl could get.

I came home to a message from my agent that the final call-back was re-scheduled a good two weeks later. I had time to recover from intense jet lag and bask in this personal turning point. I would also learn that the audition was scheduled hours before my gig to launch the third album, *Powder Blue*, with my band in the East Village. This was crazy and somehow just right. One case of nerves neutralized the other. When I was tempted to panic about my singing voice, I focused on my selling script. When combating a case of audition anxiety, I had to transport boxes of CDs to the SideWalk Cafe. The stars were aligned in such a way that I couldn't get in my own way in either scenario.

I was surrounded by the final candidates for the job. There was the blond, the red head, the one who looked truly Italian, and me. What was interesting was I was overhearing some of them question how they would fulfill the demands of home shopping with their acting and music careers. One of the candidates actually brought her latest album in to the audition to share with the decision-makers behind the casting door. I understood sales, and I understood cosmetics. They don't want to hear about acting, singing, or anything other than expanding their business, and rightfully so. What did I bring? I brought in my cosmetic and sales resume and responded, "Yes, I am ready to make a complete commitment to your business. No, I don't act anymore." When they asked about my performance past, I told them that I make music on the side.

After I applied Sal's selling adjustments to my second and final take, the people behind the desk seemed pleased. All I knew was that I had done my absolute best and was relieved that I didn't have the usual time to second guess all I did in that room. I had a show to do! I ran home to remove my pin stripe suit, don my singer-songwriter blue jeans, and taxi downtown in time for the sound check.

So, I got the job. As my agent began to negotiate this trial run in Canada, I began training with Sal. The office was located on Madison Avenue, and the lovely receptionist escorted me to the conference room where I marveled at the clear glass shelves and all the bath and body flavors I was now to promote. This was my ideal kid-in-the-candy shop experience. After Sal filled my brain with all the selling tips that worked for him, he said, "Feel free to take whatever you want home to help you prepare." Soon I was barreling across town with shopping bag upon shopping bag of delicious-smelling creams, lotions and potions. I was in heaven, I was totally sold. These products were extraordinary. I loved bath and body! Who knew? Jay wasn't going to have shelf space in our bathroom ever again.

When they flew me down to observe Sal and Angela selling the brand "live", I panicked. When I passed the products lining the walls, carts of jewelry, and the racks of rain coats waiting in the wings to be sold on the American channel that day, I was overwhelmed. Like when I was first sent away to sleep-away camp, I needed a pep talk from Mom. I snuck away to call her in NYC from a pay phone, collect. How Mom knew just what to say in that moment still amazes me. "Margaret Hall Flather, do you realize how many thousands of women you can reach through this medium, the hope you can give, the self-esteem you can improve? When it is your turn to sell that skin care, you go out there and sell those products as honestly and as intelligently as you can." Spot on, Mom. Spot on.

The night before Sal, Angela and I were to launch, the three of us were brainstorming over dinner in the hotel dining room. Here was the problem. How was I to be introduced? I needed a title. I needed to show all of Canada that I was an expert. I had to be something like Director of Training and Development. I couldn't be Meg. That was too casual, so I became Margaret, Director of Training and Development. The only one to call me Margaret was my father, complete with his heavy Bostonian accent. The next day on air, every time someone referred to me as Margaret, Director of Training and Development, I had no clue who they were talking about. Then in a flash, I remembered that I was Margaret and jumped in with, "Yes, now what were you saying?" It was truly comical.

On the launch morning, we figured that it would be a Sal and Angela-based show, with Margaret, Director of Training and Development, joining the show in the last twenty minutes. The hosts were incredible. They had to manage three personalities behind their selling desk, while effectively communicating the price, shipping and product details in succinct and entertaining ways. After the first day of shows, most of the kits were sold, and the Italians and the Canadians were thrilled to join forces.

The next day, Sal thought it was time to throw me in the water without a paddle once and for all. "No one is ever ready, Meg. You learn this skill on your feet." We had one show at 9 p.m. left. Sal said that Angela would sit this one out and that I would occupy her chair. I knew that this was deciding time. The buyers, programmers, and powers that be would now decide if I was strong enough to carry this line, with Sal only stepping in when I needed him to.

At our dinner break before this live audition before all of Canada, Angela neutralized much of my fear. Her warm soul found its way through her eyes to fill me with all the confidence and purpose I needed. Angela had many mysterious, extraordinary gifts, she even read my palms. What secrets did she discover while combing the lines in my right hand with her perfectly manicured fingers? That I would travel internationally through work and thrive. As we all got into the car to drive back to the channel, silently from the back seat, I kept channeling the Meg that Angela saw and the professional travels she was certain I would take. My adrenaline pumped as we pulled into the parking lot. I briefly shut my eyes, trying to imagine myself curled up beneath Angela's certainty, tucked in tight for the night by this mentor, teacher, and friend.

Susan was to be our host. As she entered the dressing room to talk through the show order, her dreamy green eyes almost purred as we first shook hands. As I nervously filled the silence, her purring pools took full inventory of my being, identifying and then understanding my every trial, demanding the very best of me. This blonde mermaid in heels would carry me through the 9 p.m. show effortlessly, taking no credit for the win. This is how Susan lives. This is who Susan is. She is a healer or sorts. She is "in" it not "of" it. She excels in the medium of television sales in order to lift others, helping them actualize what they want and giving them what they don't know they need. Between Angela's palm reading and Susan's empowering purr, I was fearless as we rounded the hallway corridor, to enter the set.

In this huge, warehouse of a room I would spot the fully functioning kitchen, the living room, the spa, the fashion runway and the ornate desk prepared to sell jewelry the hour following our show. The producer's desk, three cameras and a television monitor stood before me as I found my middle stool, to begin this maiden voyage.

Since I was still learning the product line and the language used to describe products on television, Susan and Sal let me lead where they knew I was strong and took hold of the reins where they knew I needed practice. Susan knew just what questions to throw me, when to expand on what I offered and when to gently steer the conversation away from one of my clunkers, (those nervous tangents I can go on that confuse rather than assist a shopper to make the right product choice). Sal's sharp sense of humor and play created a fun banter between us while he made clear points. Sal was particularly good at talking the value. How "Picking up this 16.8 ounce costs less that buying two 8.4 ounces, and in the USA this cream here is sold in stores for $30 dollars!"

With no rehearsal, script or opportunity to look at my cheat sheets, this hour that was to determine my future just worked. It clicked on every level. We sold out of every item by the end of the hour, securing ourselves as proud new vendors, and I officially became Margaret, Director of Training and Development. Some may say the stars were aligned that night. I would say I was sent angels named Sal and Angela from New Jersey, and Susan from Toronto.

Let Him Love You

It's bitter and breezy
A blizzard in spring
Shadows in morning
What weather will bring

Alone and together
Where back roads meet
Calm and crazy
Settled and incomplete

Let him love you
He's the man that loves you
He's that one that shows up
When the rest disappear
After all the tries
With all the other guys
He's the man that loves you
And looks to your eyes

Those well meaning worriers
Scare and scold
Committed to an office chair
Setting goals

A leap of faith
Is not a leap that's safe
Up and off the fence
You can't have both ways

Let him love you
He's the man that loves you
He's that one that shows up
When the rest disappear
After all the tries
With all the other guys

He's the man that loves you
And looks to your eyes

He won't compete
With the fantasy
The painted pose
Of how it's supposed to be
Who ever said
That love is sweet?
You want a love so real
Not a love so neat
Mess it up! Mess it up!

I know you're tired, so tired
Never going deeper
Up against the edge
Toes in the water

Jump in, jump in
You want to swim
Into the waves
Holding on to him

Let him love you
He's the man that loves you
He's that one that shows up
When the rest disappear
After all the tries
With all the other guys
He's the man that loves you
And looks to your eyes
For an answer

It's bitter and breezy
A blizzard in spring
What's the answer?

Shadows in morning
What weather will bring
What's the answer?

Let him love you
Let him love you

Chapter Twenty-nine

"I am Meg."

So, after the dust and contract negotiations were settled, it was time for Meg to fly solo in Canada. Sal had come for one final visit in January to complete his passing of the ball and Angela joined me for one final hour to do the same. The shoppers showed up for my shows with Sal and Angela, but would they show up for me flying solo? The channel had warned me that bath and body as a category had never really succeeded before. Canadians are very practical, no nonsense people. They part with their money only and I mean only if it makes good, common sense to. I had to really make my case why anyone should spend $24.50 for 16.8 ounces of body cleanser, but I was determined to do it. But something was off. Something in my on-air persona needed to be corrected.

As I studied home shopping, talk shows and news broadcasts in general, I began to realize that the key to winning over your audience is to truly, and I mean truly, be yourself. Oprah had been so brave to share her childhood demons of sexual abuse and her continual struggle with weight. I needed to come clean with my viewers. I needed to be Meg.

There is a constant lesson that runs like a red thread through the tapestry of my life. That theme or thread has been my willingness to imitate another's look, voice and style, rather than challenge my essence to surface and engage. To listen to voices within that tell me what I have to offer is not special, unique or compelling enough. The beauty of home shopping is that it does not work if the shopper can't feel you, you. Unlike performing a musical on a Summer Stock stage or squeezing toilet paper in a taped commercial, you know right away if you have successfully connected with your shopper. She either picks up the phone to buy what you are selling or she changes the channel. It is all cut and dry, black and white. And what a gift that is? What an opportunity for me to wrestle my red threaded demon to the ground and win the battle, once and for all!

Once and for all I had to be myself. I had to be. The exchange of goods and services was not going to take place unless I brought all of Meg, all of Meg to that camera lens. As I entered the studio on that first solo visit with Sal and Angela back in their busy lives and the company suits tucked in safe behind desks in the Madison Avenue office, I heard Lana's voice chant in mind, "Take off the mask. Take off the mask, Meg."

The host began the sell. She shared the item number, shipping and handling charges being offered, and then passed the ball to me. Instead of jumping right in to my "We began over 70 years ago as a leading pharmaceutical house specializing in the cultivation of medicinal plants," I instead looked straight in to the camera and said something like, "OK, I need to say something. I am Meg. The only person who calls me Margaret is my father. Meg from New York City. I live in an apartment the size of a litter box with my fiancé and our twelve year old cat. I also am not Director of Training and Development. I mean I'd like to be someday, but I am not that yet. I am a shop girl of sorts and I have sold cosmetics most of my adult life. It brings me so much joy to empower women and build their self-esteem with quality products that treat their skin, their mood, their spirit. I just love these products because they do just that. They help me through my difficult city days and I believe they will do the same for you. So, call me Meg. Meg from New York City, who just like you needs a little lift from time to time."

Well, that was that. The phone lines lit up, the customers began to call me "live" on air, and I began to feel a true purpose.

With each visit we grew viewers and sales totals by considerable percentages. The company and channel management left me alone to develop my own selling style. It had to be more than talking value and reciting prepared sound bites from the company training manual. How would Oprah do it? How would Oprah promote bath products on shopping television? The answer came to me.

I would research the history of each flower, fruit, herb, nut, oil or butter being sold. It would give that "flavor" depth, dimension, a personality by sharing the fun facts, folklore, medicinal and aromatherapy history associated with that flavor. This would open up a dialogue with my shopper. I could then talk about depression, anxiety, the ups and downs of life. This would no longer be just a bath and body line that smoothed skin. These products would become a means to heal and lift the spirit. To do all this, to be myself, share my Meg story and passion for why fatty acids, amino acids and anti-oxidants are key to healthy, younger looking skin was like coming out of the darkness and in to the light. The work with Lana, all the angels that crossed my path, the numerous auditions, wins, failures, the merry go round of men that came and left, all of it was useful. All of it made perfect sense. Nothing was a mistake.

The women of Canada will never know the huge role they played in my process, my discovery. So, woman to woman, from a camera lens to a household television set, I learned never, ever doubt what is real and never take the faith and loyalty your viewing audience gives you for granted. Again, there are no coincidences. When the student is ready the teacher appears. The teacher in this case was the women of Canada, a county of angels to add to my list.

Chapter Thirty

Full Circle

Just as the lovely makeup artist dusted my face with just enough loose powder, it was time. It was time for us to *click, click, click* down that corridor together to get our microphones and go to work. I had shared my story and strangely, she was moved. She was inspired. Maybe, just maybe the lessons I learned could do some good for her and other divas out there, divas everywhere? My story seemed to comfort her nerves and the pressure she was under to move product in the final hour she was to share with me. I was to sell my remaining kits in the first half of the hour, and she was to sell the very makeup she applied on my face in the second half. Lo and behold, dear Susan was waiting on the set, our host for this final hour of the day. Again, no coincidences.

The young artist stood in the darkness behind her selling table and watched me work to the right behind mine. As the lights and camera were fixed on Susan and myself, I could feel my young diva's eyes studying my spontaneous dance with Susan, my weaving of features, benefits, folklore and product demonstrations that all came so easily to me now. Susan beamed at me, quietly knowing what was going on, quietly sensing me show off just a little before my new student, project, diva. Her green eyes twinkled with a wink that seemed to say, "Remember that first show, Meg? Look at you now."

When I began to document this story, I thought for certain it was a "star to be" story of a performer who eventually "made it" in cable shopping television. I have now sold four other brands on the three networks here in the states and appeared on the shopping network of Australia and as a consultant, have trained six other spokespeople for their home shopping debuts.

But as I type, as I share with you now, I realize this is not that story.

This is not that story at all.

This is a story of the necessary failures, missteps and heartaches that paved the way for successes, deep friendships, and true love. This is a story of surrender, of coming clean. It is the story of erasing old, fixed tapes of "the plan" to then allow what comes naturally to chart the course. It is about finally walking through the open door that says, "Yes" rather than pound the closed door that says, "Maybe, maybe, maybe" then most defiantly, "No."

This is a story of making lemonade out of lemons, grieving, and then letting go of the myths you spent decades, too many decades, telling yourself. Myths that demanded the body you were suppose to have, the success you were supposed to be, and man you were supposed to love.

This is a story of asking for help and being proudest of that act.

It is a story of allowing the universe to be your career coach, your agent, and your match maker.

This is a story of recognizing angels, angels who show up just when you need them, in all sizes, shapes and shades. Angels that come for a minute and angels that guide you for a lifetime.

This is a story of removing the mask, taking a hard look at the past, enduring the necessary emptiness of the present, to finally, discover, accept and thrive from who you truly are in this moment right now.

This is also a story of allowing those who see you, to help you, to love you and if you are really brave, to love yourself a bit as well.

What has this Home Shopping Diva learned? This kind of love, this kind of love is all that matters.

Love Is All That Matters*

I've collected souvenirs
Some late night break-up tears
These shadows let me go
Explaining they have seeds to sew

What am I just not getting?
Play back
What must I see?
To write the lasting ending
With someone next to me?

Love is all that matters
Love is what we crave
It's behind all of the dreaming
From the cradle to the grave
Love is all that matters anyway

I've lingered at the door
Consumed with what they say
They decide whose wings will fly
In a woven, chosen sky

Don't want to smile on cue
Or hide the secrets I've been through
Or the years around my eyes
I'm going to find what never dies

Love is all that matters
Love is what we crave
It's behind all of the dreaming
From the cradle to the grave
Love is all that matters anyway

I've followed judges
Holding grudges

Bought the ticket
And learned the speech
Plots are spinning
So fixed on winning
Grass so green
And out of reach

I'll trade in my ambition
Exchanging pots of gold
To share my silver hair
As I grow old

Willing heart, you keep on ticking
Patiently
Without a break
Now one more risk
I ask you take

Love is all that matters
Love is what we crave
It's behind all of the dreaming
From the cradle to the grave

Love is all that matters
Love is what we crave
It's behind all of the dreaming
From the cradle to the grave
Love is all that matters anyway

Love is all that matters
Love is all that matters anyway
Love is all that matters
Love is all that matters anyway
Love is all that matters

All of Meg's original music is available on iTunes